Success with Houseplants

Success with Houseplants

The Down-to-Earth Guide to Indoor Foliage Plants

Chuck Crandall

Chronicle Books

Dedication

For Bee Gee, who developed a love for green growing things akin to mine, and who selflessly sacrificed many treasured kitchen utensils and sink space to help advance my horticultural explorations.

Acknowledgements

Special thanks to my consultant, Professor David G. Dixon, Associate Professor of Biology and Chairman of the Department of Life Sciences, Los Angeles Valley College. I am indebted, also, to Dr. James L. Campbell, Associate Professor of Biology, Los Angeles Valley College, the Shinkles of Valley Garden Supply, No. Hollywood, and George Giebel, Mordigan Nurseries, for help in acquiring many of the more exotic specimens which appear in this book.

Copyright ©1974 by Chuck Crandall

Printed in the United States of America.

ISBN 0-87701-067-6

Library of Congress Catalog Card No. 73-77332

Contents

Foreword   6

1   Tips on Plant Shopping   9

2   When You're Going to Pot   17

3   Water and Humidity Requirements of Houseplants   27

4   Dormancy   33

5   Soils and Soil Amendments   35

6   Fertilizers, Vitamins and Hormones   39

7   Is There a Doctor in the House?   43

8   Cacti and Other Succulents—The Water-Less Plants   53

9   Herbs—A Cook's Tour   59

10   Terrariums and Bottle Gardens   65

11   Dollar Stretchers, Miscellany 'n' Serendipity   73

12   Some Choice Houseplants and How to Grow Them   79

Glossary of Horticultural Terms   125

Bibliography   127

Index   128

Foreword

Plants are a lot like people—if you feed them when they're hungry, give them water when they're thirsty and bestow an occasional kind word, they'll respond with affection. There is no great mystery to growing showy specimens that add color, beauty and individuality to your home. The green thumb myth is just that—a myth.

Plant-lovers, I have found, are a special breed. They are, by and large, gentle and sensitive beings who share a common concern for the future of mankind. They recognize the menace that our continuing worldwide romance with rampant technology and growing apathy toward environmental pollution pose for the ecological balance of our fragile spaceship, Earth.

I would be amazed to hear, for example, of a man who grows orchids beating his wife (unless, of course, he apprehended her plucking his Cattleyas for a corsage). And, regardless of how feisty and temperamental she seems, a LOL who grows African violets in her lavender-scented bathroom could never be guilty of any misconduct more heinous than sneaking an occasional nip of the cooking sherry. If generalizations about people are valid at all then those who love plants are "trustworthy, loyal, brave, clean . . ."

To be a successful indoor gardener, the first thing you must accept is that plants are living entities which need, *on an individual basis*, light, food, water, humidity—and love. Love, let me emphasize, is important—even crucial. You must empathize with your plants. If one is not feeling well, you should be sensitive to its malaise. If a leaf is torn, you must feel—at least emotionally—some of the pain.

I am a firm believer in the contention that plants are sensitive to various stimuli; that they have "feelings" as do other living things. Serious scientific experiments have proven that plants "react" on an emotional level when injured and that harsh treatment, whether actual or implied, causes hyperactivity in their foliage. One test which was illuminating involved two plants of the same kind, both grown under identical environmental conditions. One plant was treated to continuous classical music, was caressed and praised lavishly. The other was left in silence, but the scientists *mentally* threatened its well-being whenever they came near it. At the end of the test period, the specimen which got the preferential treatment was thriving magnificently; the one subjected to mental malevolence was stunted and rather pathetic-looking. (You can find parallels in the human and animal species.)

Another significant factor you should always keep in mind is that plants are individuals—even two from the same mother plant are different. You simply cannot treat two plants alike. Water, light, and feeding requirements vary from specimen to specimen. Some of my more demonstrative horticultural friends even have names for each of their plants. When they arise in the morning it's "Good morning, Roger. How did you sleep, Brenda?" Well, why not? Their collections are doing splendidly.

While I don't call my plants by name, I do talk to them and I frequently play Vivaldi and Scarlatti for them. (I don't know if they prefer Baroque to "heavy" classical fare, but I do.)

A third point, before you plunge headlong into indoor gardening, is to accept the fact that plants do make some demands upon your time. The larger your collections, the more time you must invest. If you're not willing to share yourself with your plants, perhaps you should collect shells or matchbooks, instead. There are few horticultural tragedies worse than an expensive, once-beautiful plant languishing from neglect.

Indoor gardening isn't really all that laborious and time-consuming, though. Five to ten minutes of care a day is usually all that's required—misting this one, grooming that one, checking for disease or pest infestation. Occasionally, more dedication is needed—repotting a pot-bound specimen, preparing your collection to survive neglect while you're on vacation, or eradicating an invasion of mealybugs.

Finally, learn to call your plants by their proper horticultural names. This seems to be a stumbling block for many novice plant lovers, and I suspect it's because they don't want to appear pretentious. Instead of calling their *Ficus elastica* a *Ficus elastica*, they refer to it as a rubber tree plant; their *dieffenbachia* becomes a mother-in-law's tongue, and so on.

Nurserymen and professional horticulturalists will treat you with more deference if you ask for a plant by its proper Latin designation. If you can't bring yourself to use the botanical names of your plants, at least commit them to memory so you can use a horticultural reference book intelligently.

Few things in life return so much for so little invested, as do plants, If you buy wisely (See Chapter I) you can acquire much-sought-after specimens very reasonably. You don't need a greenhouse or potting shed to grow and care for the most exotic of specimens. You can grow some fine foliage varieties even in the stygian darkness of a windowless city apartment. In return for your investment, you'll get a chance to commune with nature on a very personal level. Your plants will take in the dry, stale air of your home and give you plenty of oxygen in exchange.

Chuck Crandall

8

Chapter 1

Tips On Plant Shopping

Before you buy. Today, let's say, you're ready to adopt a beautiful plant. Great! But, before you spend your hard-earned money, you should ask yourself this important question: Can I provide the right environment and light level for this plant? If you can't answer this question, you shouldn't head for the plant shop yet.

How often have you bought a plant that was lush and healthy, then watched helplessly over the next few weeks as it steadily deteriorated into a naked stem? Tragic, wasn't it? You may have tried water or withheld it; perhaps, you gave it extra fertilizer or hormones; you may even have set it outside for a "revitalizing" sunbath. And, in the end, you still lost the battle.

You may have chalked all this up to your lack of a green thumb; to be brutally frank, it was your lack of basic horticultural savvy that did it. In this book, and dozens of others like it, you'll find probably more information than you care to know on providing the ideal care and environment for hundreds of plants, shrubs and trees. Zero in on those for which you can provide the required growing conditions, then go out and shop for that new specimen. Armed with the knowledge of it's characteristic requirements and growth habits, you'll know exactly what the plant needs to thrive and what you can expect from it.

If you do buy a plant on impulse, talk to someone there who seems knowledgeable about plants. Describe the conditons you can provide and ask him or her how the plant will fare in the location you have in mind. It would really be wise (and your new plant would appreciate it) to go to a book store or library and look the plant up in a copy of "EXOTICA," the definitive horticultural reference on tropical and subtropical plants. If you can't give the plant the environment it needs, why risk your money? Settle for something less desirable which can adjust easily in your home.

When you're browsing through plant shops and nurseries, don't be misled by the present surrounding in which a plant may apparently be thriving. A large-foliage plant in the middle of a boutique floor, for example, may appear to be growing well in the dim light, but chances are it hasn't been there very long. The shop owner may be rotating plants, moving them closer to the window or other light source for a few days, then back to the lower light level, and so on. You've got to do your research, either by reading or asking questions, on every new plant you want to buy, if you want to succeed with plants indoors.

What about those magnificent large-foliage plants you see in dim light in shopping centers and office building lobbies? This is often an illusion, too. Most of these specimens were acclimated over a period of months —even years—by the grower to survive in dim light. The others are replaced on a regular basis, usually every two weeks, by the planting contractor.

If money is a consideration, you should bear in mind that there are three things which determine the price of a plant: (1) Availability, (2) size, and (3) the type of outlet offering the plant. Many of the more desirable specimens are in short supply, particularly in the northern states where nearly all houseplants must be hothouse grown because of the short growing season and intemperate climate. A few of these are *Dracaena marginata* (sometimes called dragon tree); *Ficus benjamina* (weeping fig); *Ficus lyrata* or *padurata* (fiddleleaf fig), and *Schefflera* (umbrella tree). These, along with a few others, are currently in vogue with interior designers and architects for installation in executive suites, banks and office lobbies. Regardless of how many of these sought-after specimens the growers produce, there are never enough of significant size to supply the demand.

Money figures into the picture, as you may have guessed. Selling to large-scale consumers is more profitable than selling to low-volume consumers, and growers often get a larger price for their more desirable stock. Like most things in the world of commerce, money talks. Large, expensive "status" plants don't move well in most nurseries and shops simply because of the high price tags. So, you should remember that it is axiomatic that the greater the size of the plant, the dearer the price.

Most of us who are serious collectors of plants really don't want to settle for the small windowsill specimens; we want the largest, lushest specimens we can acquire or, in some cases, accommodate in the limited interior space available in tiny city apartments. Those of us who are weary of the traditional standbys—*Dieffenbachia, Monstera deliciosa* (split-leaf philodendron), *Ficus decora* (rubber tree)—can expect to pay between $60 and $100 for a more exotic variety large enough to get excited about.

The alternative to paying a premium price for an uncommon specimen has less aesthetic appeal, but is better than nothing at all, Buy three smaller plants, preferably of varying heights, and pot them up in one container. Eventually, you have the kind of showcase specimen you want, but resign yourself to the fact that it often takes years to achieve this effect. It took, for example, four years for me to get five feet of height from four *Dracaena warneckii* plants that were only a foot tall at the outset.

If this is what you're after—a focal-point rather than an accent plant—and you are willing to endure the wait, don't persuade yourself you can do it with a single plant. With the exception of a very few varieties (and, even then, only with some expert doctoring), houseplants do not branch or throw new plants, known as suckers or offsets. A single-stemmed plant, regardless of height, seldom makes an attractive display.

You should be mindful that there is usually a wide variance in price between the various plant outlets. Plant shops located in a high-rent building or in an area of town patronized largely by tourists, frequently mark up their stock to compensate for their high overhead. Until you've gained some knowledge of what a fair price for a given specimen should be, do a bit of comparison shopping. Snoop around several outlets in different parts of town and check the price tags. By doing this, you can often stretch your plant dollar two to three hundred percent.

When to buy. You can buy indoor foliage plants any time of year, but your best time is in early spring. You'll be getting fresh stock from the grower which is ready to take off. Spring is the beginning of the growing season for indoor plants, too, and a plant that is thriving can take the shock of repotting and adjusting to your interior in stride.

Although there's no hard-fast rule against buying a new plant in mid-winter, it may not care much for the hot, stuffy interior of a furnace-heated environment or the short, dull days and frigid nights.

Lastly, nurseries and other retailers of plants begin getting stock in quantity in spring, so your selection and the price you'll have to pay will both be better beginning in April in temperate portions of the country and May elsewhere.

What to buy. You may be limited in your choice of plants if you live in a rural or wilderness area, but even those of you who do can still acquire unusual specimens through the mail. Those of you who live in or near a metropolitan area have an almost unlimited selection of tropicals and subtropicals from which to choose.

If you're a newcomer to plant collecting, you should start out with those plants which are noted for their hardiness and ability to cope with adverse conditions or, in some cases, with indifferent care. A few of these are: *Agave*, asparagus ferns, *Beaucarnea recurvata* (pony tail or bottle palm), *Cissus antarctica* (kangaroo vine) and *C. rhombifolia* (grape ivy), *Euphorbia Milii* (crown of thorns), *Dieffenbachia* (dumb cane), *Dracaena* (virtually all varieties), *Ficus* (again, virtually all members of the fig family, but *F. decora*, or rubber tree, in particular), *Howea belmoreana* (Kentia palm), *Pittosporum Tobira* (Australian laurel or mock orange), and *Sansevieria* (snake plant). Add to this list most succulents, from jade tree to sedum, and cacti, if you have a sunny spot which will accommodate these.

You'd be wise—at least for a while—to avoid those plants which require specialized care or pampering. This list would include: *Araucaria excelsa* (Norfolk Island pine), *Cycas revoluta* (Sago palm), *Cyclamen*, *Fuchsia*, gardenia, *Helxine Soleirolii* (baby tears), *Ixora* (jungle flame), and orchid. Add in nearly all ferns, particularly *Nephrolepsis exaltata* (Boston fern), but exclude the easy-care asparagus species which are not technically ferns at all.

Should you get the baby or the mother? This is largely a matter of personal taste and the state of your finances. Some people like a lot of small plants; others prefer a few large ones. Obviously, smaller plants make a less noticeable dent in your pocketbook and (heaven forbid!) if the plant fails, you're not out a lot of *pesos*.

While I am inclined to seek out the largest (i.e., oldest) plants to adopt, there are drawbacks in this for those who can't or aren't disposed to invest some extra time in acclimating the plant. A traditional greenhouse-grown specimen that has been thriving for three or four years in the controlled environment of a greenhouse is pretty much set in its ways. The older the plant, the more un-reasonable it may be when you try to adapt it to your interior. There's simply no way of escaping problems with moving a plant such as this to a radically-different environment.

High humidity is the primary requirement. In the greenhouse, the plant lived in a humidity level of around 80%. Outside the hothouse, there is no practical way you can attain this air moisture content, but you can increase the humidity a few percentages, and a little is better than nothing at all. You can do this by giving the plant frequent mistings of water vapor from an atomizer and you might also set the plant on a saucer or tray filled with pebbles over which you've poured a little water.

Adequate light to duplicate the intensities which existed in the greenhouse is difficult to achieve, since few of us have skylights, Even so, an established plant may accept a location which gets natural light from two directions.

Although all this sounds discouraging, you can acclimate an older plant with patience and care, but you shouldn't expect it to look as beautiful and hardy as it did the day you brought it home. Dropped foliage and browned-off leaf tips will never be replaced. In a few months, though, it should adapt to its new surroundings and begin to thrive again.

If all this still seems a bit too formidable, you may want to start with a smaller, juvenile plant or tree. Generally, the younger the plant, the easier it is to acclimate it. Like a child, it is more resilient and bounces back more readily from abuses and unfavorable conditions than a mature specimen. Then, too, there's the monetary consideration. Your outlay is going to be much smaller for a juvenile than for an adult, as I've said. Remember, though, that you've got a long wait ahead before your new baby will be large enough to fill that empty corner. Very few plants grow rapidly in the adverse conditions of the typical home or apartment. *Dieffenbachia* (dumb cane), *Ficus decora* (rubber tree), *Philodendron selloum* (tree or saddle-leaf philodendron), and *Brassaia actinophylla* (schefflera or umbrella tree) are four of the commonly available specimens which will grow impressively indoors—as much as three feet in a year.

Where to buy. There are three primary retail outlets for houseplants: (1) Supermarkets, (2) plant boutiques or florists, and (3) nurseries.

The *supermarket* plant and flower department is a relatively new development. Most markets started out by offering some really unbelievable plastic monstrosities, and —proving the old axiom, "Nobody ever lost money underestimating the taste of the public"—many people bought them. (Look, Marge, and you don't have to water them!) Seeing the potential in a good thing, the markets added a selection of popular houseplants and floral specimens. Now, shoppers can buy their plants along with their groceries and save a trip to the nursery, or so the markets say. On the surface, this seems to make a lot of sense. But, for the most part, supermarket plants are a cruel hoax on the unwary shopper. Most markets which operate their own plant and flower department obviously know little and care less about plant culture. A spot check of several supermarket plant departments over a two-month period turned up cases of spider mite, mealybug and scale infestations which eventually would affect every plant on display. Market plants are apparently doused with water once a day. (They always seem to be sitting in a tray of water.) To compound the tragedy, they're (1) potted up without crocking for good drainage, (2) in plastic pots which keep the soil wet and soggy, and (3) smothered in layers of foil which hasten the drowning process by holding in excess water. The *coup de grâce* is the inflated price. Dish garden plants which sell everywhere else for 39¢ go for 99¢. Boston ferns in four-inch pots which are almost universally available at $2.95 to $3.25 fetch nearly double these prices at the neighbor-hood chain market. Virtually every specimen, no matter how common, is marked up twice or three times what a reputable nursery would charge for the same plant—in good condition.

There are some markets with a plant/flower department operated as a concession by a local nursery. Usually, the selection is greater and the specimens seem much healthier, since they are serviced by the concessionaire, instead of mauled by the market's slack-jawed stockboy. The only drawbacks I can see to purchasing these plants are (1) they're usually overpriced by as much as three dollars and (2) they are often somewhat shop-worn from rough treatment at the hands of that ubiquitous breed of shopper who must fondle, squeeze and pinch everything in the store.

Plant *boutiques* and *florists* shops specializing in the more exotic, hard-to-find specimens are ideal sources for healthy thriving plants, especially if you're not on a stringent budget. Depending upon location (high-rent district, low-rent district) and the philanthropic propensities of the owner, prices vary considerably between shops, I've seen price spreads as much as forty dollars for the same type of plant in the same type of container merely by driving across town. I've also found certain specimens in the most expensive shop in town priced ten to twenty dollars *cheaper* than the bargain outlets. There doesn't seem to be any rhyme or reason to plant pricing practices among the smaller shops. One simply has to comparison shop.

One appealing feature of the plant specialty shop is that the enterprise seems to be a labor of love. It is immediately apparent from the condition of the plants that the shop owner lavishes love and care on his "wards" and a well-adjusted plant is a happy plant. I've been in a few shops, though, where I felt the proprietor carried his stewardship to extremes by following me around and watching out of the corner of his eye to make certain I didn't molest any of his "children." You begin to sense that the owner really doesn't want to sell anything; that, perhaps, he was suddenly thrust into penury by some evil machination of the archest of villains. And, in point of fact, many of the plants on display carry boldly-lettered signs saying, "Not For Sale." You are made to feel that, if you do not provide an attractive comfortable home for the plant, the shop owner may swoop down on you in the middle of the night and reclaim it.

Some of the more dedicated shop owners do what nurseries should but seldom do: identify their plants by genus and provide a small card which contains ample data on basic care for each specimen.

If it were not such a costly venture, I would purchase all my plants from a good plant boutique. It is obvious that the owner chose his low-volume pursuit out of love for growing things, unlike the high volume nurseryman who views himself as a businessman and his plants as a marketable commodity.

Nurseries and *garden centers*, however, are still the best place to buy plants when all factors are considered—price, selection and availability. Nurseries, as I've said, deal in volume—the plant that comes in from the wholesaler on Friday is usually sold over the weekend—and they usually prefer to sell a great many plants for less money to make their profit. Generally speaking, they don't invest the amount of time in preening and misting their stock that plant specialty shops do and, perhaps, their specimens are not quite as handsome, but you are assured of low price, good health and freedom from disease and insect infestation. If a plant turns out to be ailing from disease or parasitic insects, most nurserymen will exchange it for a healthy specimen or another plant that meets your approval. Nurseries, also, are usually the first to get new varieties and hybrids which have been developed by commercial growers and horticulturalists.

Browsing around nurseries and chatting with nurserymen can be very beneficial for novice gardeners and indoor horticulturalists. By actually seeing the plant varieties, you can decide which specimens have the most appeal for you. Books and photographs are no match for a trip to the nursery. Furthermore, by checking out several nurseries, you can get a fairly reliable barometer of price structures in your area for various specimens. While it is usually true that nurseries are the most economical source for plants, prices often vary between nurseries. A nursery in the "better" part of town or wealthy suburban community will almost always charge more for everything than one in an industrial or economically-depressed area.

Information is available at nurseries, in varying degrees of usefulness. Most nurserymen are primarily outdoor plant and tree experts and are often only vaguely knowledgeable about houseplants. A few nurseries have an interior plant department and extensive houseplant inventories in infinite variety. The staff who run this department are often professional horticulturalists or, at least, laymen experts, who seem well informed on houseplant culture, down to the most minute detail. There are usually pamphlets and booklets available on houseplant care, sometimes prepared by the state nurserymen's association, sometimes by manufacturers of gardening products. These can be a goldmine of helpful information and, best of all, they are usually free.

Then, there are nurseries whose proprietors view the houseplant buyer as a nuisance—someone who just gets underfoot and is forever asking inane questions. Like many businessmen, they are primarily concerned with the Big Sale. If you're not planning to landscape your yard, they seem icily aloof or rude and gruff.

Fortunately, most nurserymen are helpful and generous with their time, regardless of the amount of the sale involved or the seeming stupidity of the questions.

There are also some good secondary

sources for plants which are available to you, provided you live in or near a large city. First of all, there are the *botanical gardens* or arboretums which usually have annual or semi-annual sales of specimen plants, some of which are quite unusual. These sales are open to the public and provide the organizations with funds for new purchases. The plants offered aren't rejects or inferior stock, but are usually specimens which are being moved out to make room for new acquisitions or which were propagated in the gardens for the purpose of the sale. Prices are moderate, comparable to what you'd pay in a good plant shop. A call to your local botanical garden will get you all the information you need —sale date, type of plants to be sold, average prices, and so on.

Plant societies, usually devoted to the propagation and cultivation of one species (orchids, for example), and *garden clubs* frequently hold shows and sales throughout the year. These events are traditionally announced in the newspaper the week before they are scheduled, but—again—a phone call will get you advance information.

Department stores, variety outlets (Wool-worth's, Kress, Kresge, Newberry, etc.) and even *building supply firms* have all jumped onto the plant retailing bandwagon. Occasionally, you can find some bargains here, particularly if you shop carefully and stick to the smaller plants.

How to buy. If you're a babe in the woods when it comes to plants, how do you know what to look for in a plant? I'm glad you asked that question. First of all, only consider plants that are obviously in good health and growing well. Even if you know next to nothing about plants you can tell just by looking at a specimen whether it's thriving or failing. A healthy plant is full of thick, deep-green bushy growth. The foliage stands out somewhat from the stem and the leaves are more or less uniform in size, except for the new leaves on top which haven't matured. There will be little or no evidence of pruning, either of stems or leaf tips, and there will be no gaps between foliage on the stem where leaves have been lost.

You should be able to see new leaf buds about to open or at least well-formed. If the growing tips are brown or black, the plant was probably sent into shock when it was potted up or from some other trauma. It may recover, eventually, but you'd be wise to pass it up. It may not revive. You should be aware that incipient disease and/or insect infestation may not be visible. A plant may have been treated for aphids or mealybugs a few days before your arrival and, while the adult parasites which are visible to the naked eye may have been eradicated, some of the tiny eggs may still be hidden in the foliage. For this reason, it's always a good idea to isolate a newly-acquired plant for a couple of weeks and keep an eye on it. Don't forget to check the undersides of leaves—this is where all houseplant parasites love to congregate and hatch new broods.

Generally, though, a plant in trouble is just as easy to recognize as a plant that is thriving. The foliage of a sick plant takes on a mangy or chlorotic (yellowish) look and hangs limp-

Choose a plant for thickness of trunk or stem.

ly, close to the stem. The leaves may be flecked with brown, yellow or red spots and new leaves may be deformed and tinged with brown. Browned-off leaf tips usually mean the plant wasn't given a high enough humidity level but can also indicate root burn from excessive fertilizer unwisely used to bring the plant along too rapidly. While we're at this point, make a mental note to always dissolve the excess fertilizer in the soil of every plant you buy and flush it out of the pot. You do this by pouring in two or three cups of lukewarm water, waiting fifteen to thirty minutes, then pouring in several cups. This will prevent fertilizer build-up in the soil and white stains on your clay pots.

I strongly recommend that you never, regardless of how large the discount, buy a sick or insect-infested plant, unless it will be the only plant in your home. There is too great a risk of contagion among the rest of your collection. If you're so bargain-conscious or so imbued with Florence Nightingale tendencies that you must have an ailing plant, by all means keep it totally isolated, use a separate watering can, and always wash your hands after handling it before touching your other specimens, until it is healthy again.

What else should you look for when selecting a plant? Assuming you've found a group of likely-looking candidates, you can get a lot more for you money by being observant. For example, if you're looking for a particular plant, check every one of that variety in the nursery's stock. Usually, they're grouped in one section, all in the same size pot. Although they all seem similar, some are different. Out of a group of 30 specimens, there may be two with more than one plant in the pot. This means a fuller plant later on and is a much better buy. Or, all but one may have stems about the same thickness. That particular one will have a trunk twice or three times as thick. This is the one to buy; it's a more mature plant and can survive changes in habitat, repotting, etc., much easier.

Another factor to consider is what kind of container the plant is potted in. Specimens offered in cans are usually less expensive, and if you have a large inventory of empty pots at home, this is the way to buy your plants. If not, and you can get the specimen either potted or in the can, compare the higher cost of the potted plant against the expenditure for a pot and soil, plus the time required. You may decide you'll save money and time by buying the specimen already potted. Before you make a commitment, though, check the drainage hole to determine if the plant is crocked. (See "Drainage," Chapter II.) If it isn't, you're going to have to repot anyway, so buy the canned specimen.

Tips on Plant Buying
1. Go for thickness in trunk or stem instead of dense foliage or height. The thicker the trunk, the more mature and well-established the plant, and the better its chances of surviving repotting and readjustment.
2. Select a plant with a good branching structure or one with more than one plant in the pot. As the plant matures, you'll have a fuller, more attractive specimen.
3. Never buy a sick plant or one obviously infested with pests, even at a marked-down price. A badly infested plant is probably already doomed and, by bringing it into your home, you may be endangering your other specimens.
4. If available, buy a plant in the can instead of the pot—you'll usually pay less. If you do buy a potted plant, check to see if it's crocked. If not, point this out to the proprietor. A consistent campaign by indoor gardeners may someday be effective in persuading growers to crock every specimen they pot up for sale.
5. Avoid seriously pot-bound plants. Check the drainage hole and, if you can see roots pushing out, it's pot-bound. This means immediate repotting is necessary or even that the plant may be on the verge of collapse because of damage to its delicate feeder roots.

Chapter 2

When You're Going To Pot

If you intend to raise beautiful plants, one of the first tasks you must master is "potting up" and "potting on" (moving up to a larger pot) your specimens. Healthy, fast-growing plants usually need larger quarters once a year to continue to flourish. Some plants you buy from shops and nurseries will probably be pot-bound, uncrocked, or in unsuitable containers. All of these conditions call for immediate remedial action.

Few things make the inexperienced indoor gardener more apprehensive than the prospect of potting up a plant. He would almost rather fight off an invasion of red spider mites than attempt repotting. Potting doesn't really deserve all this ferment—it's one of the simplest horticultural jobs. It's like learning to ride a bicycle. After you've done it once, you never forget how.

When to pot. The most auspicious time to pot is spring. Even though houseplants are acclimated to an artificial environment where the thermostat maintains a fairly constant temperature, they still are more or less inclined to follow the seasons in their growth habits. The arrival of spring seems to signal a time for rejuvenation, and root activity begins in earnest, only to slow down again with the advent of shorter days in the fall.

Actually, you can repot successfully any time of year (provided a plant is not in dormancy; *see Index*). The odds are more in your favor in the peak of the growing season, but a broken pot or a recently-acquired specimen that is severely pot-bound can't wait until spring.

A pot-bound plant is easily recognized. The first signs may be yellowing, then loss of the lower leaves. Eventually, the roots begin to shoot out of the drainage hole in the base of the pot. Some plants even push up out of their containers to signal for help. The roots have used up all the growing room inside the pot (and most of the soil and nutrients, too) and are frantically searching for more.

The lifeline of a plant springs from the delicate feeder roots which nourish the plant. These are the tiny hair-like roots near the end of every root. When these are exposed outside the protection of the pot—as occurs when the roots are allowed to escape through the drainage hole—they can be mortally damaged, sending the plant into shock and ultimately causing death.

Many commercial growers keep their plants in a pot-bound condition because "root-crowding" (growing a plant in a container too small for its root structure), like "pinching out" (*See Glossary*), is often a successful method of keeping a specimen lush and full—for a time. The grower's goal is to deliver to his buyers full-foliage specimens which are more attractive to the public. The danger lies in allowing a plant to remain severely pot-bound for an extended period. Eventually, the plant depletes the food supply in the soil and either succumbs from malnutrition or root damage.

Plants in pots are not in nature's scheme of things. Every natural function of the plant is unnaturally controlled—even photosynthesis (conversion of energy to food—see Glossary for full explanation) is affected to some degree. The confines of the pot dictate where and how extensively the roots may grow; water is given or withheld, often on caprice rather than need; light is usually inadequate; heat is artificial and excessive; and humidity almost non-existent. It seems a miracle that a plant survives indoors at all.

Drainage. Although a plant can and usually does overcome man-made obstacles to its

Pinching out growing tips occasionally promotes fuller, bushier specimens.

survival, one thing it must have is an efficient water drainage system. All plants, whether they're growing naturally or in pots, need good drainage or their roots will rot. Drainage is even more critical to the well-being of plants confined in containers which hinder natural evaporation of moisture, such as plastic or ceramic. Soil composition, which will be discussed later, is an important factor in efficient drainage, but the most important element is the drainage hole—it must be kept open and free of obstructions, so that excess water can pass through the soil rapidly. This is where *crocking* comes in.

Crocking material is exactly what the name implies—old crocks, or clay pots which are broken into chunks about three inches long (although you can use rocks). A layer of crocking (about one inch deep) should be the first thing that goes into a pot, followed by a

good soil mixture suitable for the plant. Don't be afraid to put crocking right over the drainage hole. Use a curved shard that arches over the hole so that water can still escape.

Let's take the potting technique step by step, to bring everything into clearer focus. First, let's examine pots themselves.

Pots. There are nine kinds of plant containers currently on the market: terra cotta (unglazed clay), ceramic (or glazed), rigid plastic, flexible (rubberized) plastic, wood, styrofoam, peat moss, metal, and wire baskets lined with sphagnum moss.

Terra cotta pots are, I feel, the best for every plant. The material is a natural earth product and is porous. Plants seem to adapt more readily to clay than any other pot material. Some indoor gardeners, particularly petite females, find the weight of clay pots a bother. There's no getting around it—clay pots are heavy. Others deplore the untidy appearance of clay pots after salts and moisture begin to leech through. There is really no solution to the problem of weight, short of keeping your cumbersome specimens on stands with casters. The obvious solutions to the last two problems are to (1) put terra cotta pots inside decorative ceramic containers or (2) occasionally scrub off the stains and algae with steel wool. This should be done periodically anyway to preserve the porosity of clay pots.

New terra cotta pots should be thoroughly immersed in water overnight then completely dried, either in the sun or a warm oven, before you plant in them. If you used an unsoaked pot, it would absorb nearly all the water you give the newlypotted plant and soil would adhere to the damp interior walls, creating problems for the feeder roots. Once a pot has been soaked or previously used, it is "seasoned" and can be used anytime thereafter without repeating the immersion process.

Old terra cotta pots are fine for potting, provided they are clean, inside and out. All dried-on soil inside must be removed with either coarse steel wool and hot water or a wire brush. If the soil is left inside when you pot up a plant, you run the risk of having the roots grow into this caked film. Then, when you attempt to knock out the plant for inspection or potting on, the feeder roots will be damaged, since the caked-on soil has become almost a part of the pot and does not release as new soil does.

Most old terra cotta pots are also coated with a patina of leeched-out salts (white stains) and a green scum (algae) which grows on these salts. The leeching process is vital to the health of a potted plant and is why pot porosity is essential. The plant is throwing off unneeded fertilizer which, if allowed to build up, may be lethal to the plant. In its natural habitat (the earth), the plant leeches excess food and water directly into the soil where they are dispersed. Only terra cotta pots are sufficiently porous to permit leeching, and this is one of the reasons I strongly recommend clay over plastic or glazed ceramic.

Glazed *ceramic* pots, like plastic, do not permit natural moisture evaporation. Their advantage over plastic is purely one of aesthetics—ceramic containers are much more attractive and are usually available in a wider range of contemporary colors and configuration. In the larger sizes, they are usually manufactured without drainage holes since they are intended to serve as decorative containers into which you set plants already in terra cotta pots. You can plant directly in ceramic pots either by drilling (or having the pottery shop or nursery do it for you) at least three holes about ¾″ in diameter in the base for good drainage, or by *dry welling*.

A dry well is a layer of rocks or crocking, at least two inches deep, preferably deeper, over which planting mix is poured. Excess water drains through the soil and down into the dry well. If there were no dry well or drainage hole, this excess water would stand in the bottom of the pot where it would sour the soil and rot the plant's roots. This is the same technique used in terrariums, which are usually set up in glass or lucite containers without drainage holes so they can be set on furniture without fear of water damage.

In theory, dry welling works splendidly; in practice, it's pretty much a hit or miss method. Since you can't, with the exception of terrariums, see where the water is going when you irrigate a dry-welled plant, you have to guess when the plant has had enough. Too much, and the dry well is useless; too little and the plant dies of dehydration.

A fairly safe guide for watering dry-welled plants—remember, this is just a guideline, not a hard-and-fast rule—give one cup of water for every inch of pot size. Pots are measured across the top, not by depth. So, a

This severely pot-bound dieffenbachia should have been potted-on months ago.

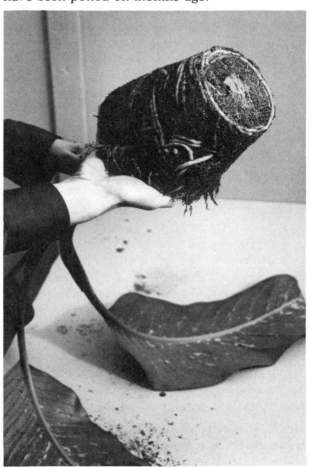

12″ dry-welled plant would get 12 cups of water. You will have to experiment for a while to hit upon the right amount of water your dry-welled plant can take, but—for safety's sake—underwater rather than drown the plant at the outset.

Rigid plastic pots are currently enjoying popularity for a number of reasons. They're lightweight, and when you get into the 12 and 14-inch containers full of soil and crocking, this is an important consideration, especially if hoisting a lot of weight isn't one of your favorite activities. They also hold in moisture eons longer than do terra cotta pots, and this is beneficial for those plants, such as the spathiphyllum, which thrive in continually moist soil. Finally, since they are non-porous, they remain relatively clean.

The latter advantage, however, can pose a problem for the inattentive indoor gardener. Since plastic is non-porous, moisture can't escape except by evaporation in the topsoil and through the drainage hole. Furthermore, you have the now-familiar leeching problem and the possibility of a plant collapse from an overabundance of salts in the soil. Continuous moisture over a long period of time can sour the soil and set up ideal conditions for root and stem rot. Since root rot is almost always fatal, it's a good idea to periodically knock out a plant potted in a plastic container and check the condition of the soil and roots. If all is well, simply slip the pot back on, right the plant and slam the base firmly against a table or counter top to reset the plant.

Some of my horticultural friends have had resounding success with gardening in plastic containers. Their specimens are luxuriant and hardy, without so much as a brown tip anywhere. On the other hand, I've had miserable results with plastic and I suspect the reason is because I'm still resisting the idea of plastic pots. I learned to grow plants in terra cotta pots years ago and am dedicated to it. If I'd started out with plastic, I probably would be just as loyal to it.

The *flexible*, or rubberized, plastic pot is a different matter. It, I fear, is a demoniac invention probably created by a mad chemist who loathes living plants. (I suspect he is also the culprit who developed those grossly offensive plastic philodendrons which plague many restaurants and doctors' reception rooms.) Because the material is non-porous, no excess moisture or salts can be eliminated by the plant, except via the drainage hole. Over and above this, the pot is too flexible and a plant simply can't take the punishment of having its root ball periodically crushed whenever the plant is moved.

Rot-resistant *cedar* and *redwood* planters and the perennially-popular soy sauce tubs are quite satisfactory as containers. They do, however, challenge your ingenuity in preventing damage to floors and carpets from the continuous contact of wet wood. You can cope with this problem by using galvanized underliners or glazed saucers under the tubs or, if you have ceramic tile or brick floors, there's no problem, at all, The obvious objection to wooden tubs is their untidy appearance. A porch or patio seems more appropriate for them, but this is your decision.

Styrofoam and *peat moss* pots are popular with many commercial growers because they are lightweight and comparatively inexpensive. When wet, both are too flexible to protect the delicate root structure of a plant and both should be used only as temporary holders, until you can pot the plant up in a conventional container. In the case of peat moss pots, you need not remove the plant; just pot it up in its peat moss container. The roots will grow through it and it will eventually break down in the soil, providing some nourishment to the plant.

Some plants are available still in the *metal* nursery can and there are now steel "decorator" pots on the market. In the first instance, you should pot up from the can when you get the plant home. In the second, you should use the steel containers only as holders for plants potted up in terra cotta pots. Metal shares the same problem as rigid plastic—a lack of porosity—which makes it unsuitable for long-term use.

Many plants, particularly ivies and other cascading plants, are well-suited to hanging *wire baskets* lined with sphagnum moss and filled with soil. Baskets and hanging devices are now commonly available at nurseries and plant shops in several sizes and ranging in price from about two to five dollars.

Whatever the composition of the pot you select to pot up your specimen, choose one no more than two inches larger than the outgrown container. If, for example, the original container is a six-inch can or pot, you should go to a seven or eight-inch container. The only time I break this rule is when I've acquired an uncrocked specimen. The crocking usually takes up so much room that I am forced to "jump" the plant. Jumping a plant means potting it in a container three or more sizes larger than the original pot. Potjumping wreaks havoc with the growing cycle of a plant. Most of the growth occurs in the root system as the plant hastens to fill up the new soil with roots and the result is only minimal top growth.

Another important point: take care to select a pot of the same configuration as the original. Many of the new faddish pots, especially the imported ones, are irregularly shaped with rim indentions that cut into the interior wall. Some taper down so sharply that it is virtually impossible to pot on a plant that is in a conventional container without inflicting serious damage on the root system or jumping the plant to a larger container.

Plastic containers are being produced in so many shapes it is difficult to keep up with them from month to month. And, one can never count on the continued availability of a particular plastic pot. If it doesn't sell well, the manufacturer may suddenly pull it off the market and introduce a new profile.

The classic shape of the traditional terra cotta pot—smooth, gradually-tapered interior wall with a thick rim that resists breaking —seems best. You can always find one a size or two larger when you're ready to pot on.

Once you've selected a pot, you're finished with the cerebral phase and are ready for the purely mechanical aspects of potting. The day before, completely saturate the plant with a Vitamin B-1 solution to prevent transplant shock. There are several brands and kindred special preparations on the market, all of which are aimed at enhancing the plant's chances of surviving the forthcoming ordeal. As you should with any solution, follow label directions precisely. Avoid the temptation to strengthen the dose; if anything, underdose.

The next step in the potting process should be to lay out the materials you will need so that you can move effortlessly from one step to the next. You will need (1) crocking for the bottom of the pot, (2) soil mix prepared in a sufficient amount to finish the job, (3) a short section of lath or a wooden rule to pack down the new soil around the root ball, and (4) a watering can filled with the recommended Vitamin B-1 diluted in water.

First, place the crocking in the bottom of the pot, then pour a half-inch layer of soil over the crocking and tamp it down. Now, you are ready to knock out the plant. Place your fingers over the rim of the pot, so that just the stem is exposed between your fingers. Invert the pot and rap the rim sharply against a solid surface, the edge of a table top, for example. The plant should slip out of its pot and drop into your hand. Before placing the plant into its new pot, gently press inward on the soil ball to keep it from collapsing. Too much pressure can damage the feeder roots. Lift the plant by placing your hands under the soil ball and set it into the pot. Make sure it's centered in the pot, then—holding the plant in place with your thumbs—pick up the pot and slam it down on any solid surface to "set" the plant in its new home. The soil level should be three-quarters of an inch to an inch below the rim, to allow room for water when you irrigate. If the soil level is lower, remove the plant and add more

Step 1. Thoroughly saturate soil the night before.

Step 4. Some horticultural charcoal in the bottom will help keep soil sweet.

Step 2. Pot should be no more than two inches larger than previous container. Measure inside rim to inside rim.

Step 5. Pour in a base layer of soil and firm.

Step 3. Layer of clay shards will keep drain hole open.

Step 6. Place hand over top of pot, as shown in illustration.

Step 7. Invert pot and rap rim sharply against a firm surface.

Plant will drop into your hand.

Step 8. Drop plant into its new pot and pour in a little soil all around the old soil ball. Make sure the plant is centered in the pot.

Step 9. Using a piece of lath or a ruler, pack down soil, add another layer, tamp it down, etc.

Step 10. The newly-potted specimen should be thoroughly watered and misted.

Plant should be centered and soil level should be half to three-quarters of an inch from the rim of the pot.

soil; if it's higher, you may have to move up to a size larger pot. All this may seem unimportant, but the value will be apparent if you attempt to water a plant that is standing too high in its pot. Furthermore, you should at least pot up your first plant correctly, so you'll know how it's done.

The next step—packing down—is crucial to the future health and survival of the plant. Plants thrive in pots (as in their natural habitat) by having soil pressed against their roots. If the new soil is too loosely packed around the old soil ball, the feeder roots simply will not penetrate into the new soil, but will continue to turn inward. This means that, while the plant may survive for a while, perhaps even indefinitely, it will never achieve the kind of luxuriant growth you desire. The soil itself also needs root activity to be oxygenated and stay in good condition.

Bruises, abrasions, splinters and the profanity they precipitate can all be avoided by wearing a gardening glove on the hand that will do the packing down. Add a little soil all around the plant and use your lath to pack it down firmly. Rotate the pot as you go to keep the plant centered. Add another layer of soil, packing as you go, then another, until the new soil reaches the level of the original soil ball. Then, water thoroughly until the excess runs out of the drainage hole. There will probably be some settling of the new soil after watering. Simply add more soil to level again. Let the newly-potted plant almost dry out before rewatering.

From time to time you may find that a plant you wish to repot requires more than the conventional repotting procedure. The old soil ball may be so packed down that all oxygen is literally being squeezed out of the soil and there may be evidence of too much insoluble salt (white stains or grey tinge) present in the soil. If this is the case, gently remove nearly all old soil from the root system. If you can, leave some of the old soil around the central root. Untangle matted roots as you go and spread them into the pot, adding new

Leeched-out salts should be removed periodically with warm water and steel wool.

soil all around. Use your tamping tool with care, so that you won't crush any roots. You still must pack soil tightly against the roots to stimulate growth, but in this case, you need a delicate touch.

What about the plant in a pot which is simply too large and heavy to knock out in the conventional manner? Since you dare not pull the plant out by its stem or trunk, or you may destroy sensitive feeder roots, or even break the stem off at the soil line, how do you get the little bugger out?

If the plant is not dry welled but potted up in a container with a drainage hole, try tipping it over (gently) on its side outdoors and forcing water up through the drainage hole with a garden hose. If this fails to loosen the soil ball, you might try a technique I've developed for extricating obstinate plants (particularly dry-welled specimens). I offer it with no guarantees. It works for me nine times out of ten, and I call it "potrolling." The preceding day, I water the plant thoroughly, and water again the next morning. I then tie up the foliage with strips cut from large plastic waste bags. These are much less destructive to the leaves than string. Next, I tip the pot over on its side and roll it across the floor. The bumping-thumping action is usually effective in freeing the plant to the point where I can ease it out of the pot. To avoid a mess, it's a good idea to spread newspaper over the trajectory the plant will take.

If this technique fails, a choice must be made between salvaging the plant or the pot. I usually sacrifice the container. This is how it's done: As always, saturate the soil the day before, then again the following day, just before you're ready to begin. Set the container on several thicknesses of newspaper and firmly rap the pot, just below the rim, with a hammer until it cracks down to the base. Repeat the process on the opposite side and the pot should fall away neatly in two pieces. Immediately repot following standard pot-ting procedures. If you get sidetracked, wrap a damp cloth or burlap bag around the soil to keep the roots from drying out.

One thing you must never do to remove a plant from its pot is to run a knife, screw-driver or anything else around the inside of the container to loosen the soil ball. This is a tempting solution to the problem when a stubborn plant won't release and you're facing the necessity of shattering a $7 container. I have even seen this recommended as S.O.P. in a few horticulture-oriented publications whose editors should know better. This is one of the most effective ways I know of to kill a plant, because the instrument used almost always cuts and rips the feeder roots and can rend the root ball beyond the resuscitative powers of the plant.

And, there you have it! Provided you stick to the basics, without deviations or shortcuts, you should pot like an expert the very first time.

Chapter 3

Water and Humidity Requirements Of Houseplants

As novice gardeners, most of us fall almost eagerly into the old trap of believing that water has some miraculous curative power which will revive a failing plant or, perhaps, even resurrect a dead one. Eight out of ten times, the very *cause* of a drooping plant's imminent collapse is our overactive watering can.

There is, of course, no question about it —plants do require water to exist, some need great quantities, others only an infinitesimal amount. How much and how frequently it is given depends upon the particular requirements of your specimens—where they are situated and the time of year. Plants in partial sun and during the summer require considerably more water than they do if they're sitting in dim light or during the winter. Cacti and succulents can get by on hardly any water seemingly forever. They have adapted admirably to their arid native environment over centuries and will soon perish if you try to make water lilies out of them. At the other end of the horticultural spectrum are the moisture-loving plants which originated in humid marshes and rainforests. The more water you give them, the better they like it, provided the excess can drain rapidly through the soil.

The most important part of any variety of plant, from a biological viewpoint, is under the surface of the soil—the root system. If the roots are unhealthy or impaired, the top growth will reflect this in a myraid of ways; ultimately, by departing for that Big Arboretum in the Sky. An adequate water supply keeps the roots active and the stems and leaves turgid and nourished. Too much water sets up root rot which is almost always fatal, if not detected in time—and it seldom is.

Soil must be given a period of drought between waterings to provide the oxygen roots need to carry on respiration. Ideally, the process takes place in this manner: As the soil begins to dry out, tiny air pockets are formed in the soil ball, and these fill with oxygen. The combination of oxygen ingestion and drying of the soil galvanizes the feeder roots into activity. They shoot out in all directions, responding to moisture, and this root action keeps the entire root structure invigorated, just as exercise contributes to our health.

A plant that has been continually overwatered always reveals certain telltale signs: There is usually a white crust on the topsoil. Many of the leaves will be browned off on the edges; those which aren't browned off will be hanging limply from moribund stems, and the soil will be standing slightly away from the interior walls of the pot. Chances are good that the soil has also soured. Soured soil has an unmistakable pungent odor, something akin to decaying onions, or worse. The roots (or what's left of them) will have a brown tinge (healthy roots are white) and will be mushy to the touch.

Since we're on the subject of soured soil and root rot, the best treatment for these maladies is to knock out the plant, remove most of the soil from around the root ball, snip away all vestiges of decayed root structure, dip the root ball in "Rootone" which has an antiseptic action, repot in fresh soil—and pray a lot. Obviously, you'll want to reappraise your watering procedures.

Since root rot is so often fatal, and is almost always brought on by overwatering, take some precautions to prevent its occurrence in your collection. When you water, always make certain your pot's drainage system is operating efficiently. Is excess water passing through the soil rapidly and escaping through the drainage hole(s)? Even a properly-crocked pot sometimes gets clogged by root masses or hardpacked soil. If you've got a plug-up, poke a stick up through the drainage hole to open the dike. Has the excess drained into the saucer and is the plant standing "up to its taproot" in water? That's a no-no! Regardless of what your Great Aunt Minnie said, this is *not* good for the plant.

Although plants, like man, have evolved into some pretty miraculous specimens, none has, so far as science can determine, learned to swim. Yet, in every hamlet in every part of the country there is a small but intensely-loyal group of "horticultural baptists" who believe, with evangelical zeal, in the Great Saucer-Watering Myth. No matter how many of their most highly-prized specimens go down for the third time to a watery grave, they remain unshakable in the belief that the only way to water a plant is by filling its saucer religiously. The sudden death of specimens and entire collections is attributed to such things as bad air, hard water or the lack of a green thumb.

As a matter of fact, it *is* beneficial for a plant to have water in its saucer, but not up to the base of the pot. The plant should be raised slightly by setting the container on a layer of pebbles, rocks, or even on a piece of wood, just as long as the base is not submerged. The evaporation of moisture from the pebbles is an effective method of raising the humidity around the plant. If you have potted plants in decorative containers, lift them out periodically to make certain they're not becoming waterlogged.

How do you determine when a plant needs water? Enough has been written on this subject to fill volumes. The most widely-accepted method, and the one I use for tropical specimens, is to insert your forefinger into the topsoil to the second joint. If the soil feels dry, water; if it's damp, don't water. When you do water, *saturate* the soil, until you can see water seeping out of the drainage hole. There are two exceptions to this rule: (1) the cacti, succulents and bromeliads, each variety of which is almost a special case, but with the emphasis on soil aridity, and (2) hanging plants and the water-loving specimens, which require almost continually moist (not wet!) soil and need daily or twice-weekly irrigation.

For those who are squeamish about getting dirt under their fingernails, or are captivated by the mystique and potential for ritual inherent in houseplant culture, there are the more exotic methods of determining when it's time to water. I mean, just any *ninny* can jab his finger into the soil and tell if it's dry—right? So, if you can't bring yourself to poke around in the soil, or you are partial to the ritualistic approach to gardening, you may want to adopt one or more of the following.

Some otherwise normal horticultural friends ceremoniously thunk the bejeebers out of their pots with spoons, trowels and sundry other implements and determine, by the hollowness of the sound, whether a plant is thirsty. Others rap hell out of their pots with their knuckles (which seems a somewhat masochistic approach to the problem). A few hardy ones hoist their specimens and deduce soil moisture content by weight.

I, personally, feel these methods are part of the folklore of houseplant culture and would not gamble the well-being of my plants on my ability to decipher the plinks and plunks of pot-thumping. I suppose, if one has finished his (or her) horticultural chores and still wants to putter around, there might be some therapeutic value in slipping the pots a couple of little thumps, just to keep a hand in, so to speak.

Water types. What kind of water is best for houseplants? Rainwater is my first choice for all my plants. It's natural and free of chemicals and earth-borne minerals, and it's a gift from nature. Those who live in environments where air pollution is a severe problem, however, should not use rainwater on their collection. Air pollutants notwithstanding, the other problem with rainwater is, of course, that there just isn't enough available. The days of the rainbarrel, like the family milk cow, alas, are gone forever. Distilled water (never artificially-softened water) is a good substitute but, as your collection of larger specimens grows, the cost can become a bit burdensome. Tapwater, even with its minerals and chemicals, is fine, unless it contains an inordinate amount of harsh chemicals, such as chlorine. If you can smell or taste chlorine in your tapwater, either let it sit overnight to allow the chlorine to evaporate or switch to bottled distilled water.

It's a good idea to let any tapwater stand for a few hours, overnight is better, to allow impurities to settle. Then, don't use the last quart or so when you irrigate.

How to water. Whatever water you prefer, bring it to room temperature (tepid) before you use it. Roots can absorb warm water much faster than cold. Excessively hot or cold water can give the plant a severe (even lethal) shock by changing the temperature around the roots too rapidly.

While there is no basis in horticultural fact, some indoor gardeners feel that any sudden rush of water from overhead irrigation is harmful to plants. They only water by dumping a tray of ice cubes on the topsoil and allowing them to melt slowly. I'm not entirely convinced that this technique isn't potentially dangerous, particularly if the stem or subsurface roots become frozen or even excessively chilled. Secondly, one would need access to a glacier to fill the water requirements of even a modest collection of large foliage specimens.

Small specimens, those in eight-inch or smaller containers, should be irrigated occasionally by completely immersing the pot in a bucket of water. This really penetrates the soil ball, right to the core, which is seldom achieved when you water in the conventional manner. Since this is a fairly messy task, I usually set aside a morning and do all my specimens—at least those I can lift—in the

Bucket-soaking is recommended every three months to thoroughly soak root ball.

bathtub. Fill the tub with lukewarm water to a point that is slightly higher than the rim of the tallest pot you'll be irrigating. One by one, immerse your pots and hold them down until they are completely soaked and stay submerged on their own. Otherwise, they'll flip over and you'll have one huge mudpack to cope with, to say nothing of broken stems and damaged foliage. Yes, some of the top soil will float out of the pots, but only a small amount which can be replaced when you're through. At this point, I turn on the shower to give the foliage a gentle warm bath for several minutes.

When the air bubbles stop rising to the surface, the pots are soaked and you can pull the plug. Needless to say, you should catch the flotsam and jetsam of bark, soil and leaves with a strainer to keep from fouling the plumbing. Let the pots drain a few minutes (in an old colander, if you have one) before returning them to their saucers.

There is also an old, time-honored watering technique which seems to have fallen by the horticultural wayside—*double-pot water-*

ing. It works only if a plant is potted up in an unglazed terra cotta container. The clay pot is placed inside another pot approximately two inches larger. Damp peat moss, which is kept moist by periodic watering, is packed loosely between the two pots and, because the terra cotta is porous, water seeps through the walls gradually, keeping the soil evenly moist. You still must irrigate the plant, but it will require water less frequently.

Double-pot watering is more effective if the outside container is plastic or glazed clay, to prevent moisture from leeching through.

You can prevent a dangerous build-up of water in dry-welled plants by laying the pot on its side after irrigating so that the excess water can seep out.

When to water. Night or morning? Since a plant's feeder roots are most active in the morning, there is a good argument in favor of a.m. watering. But, as long as the air temperature inside remains a fairly constant 70°, morning and night, either a.m. or p.m. irrigation is fine. The primary case against night watering is that the roots don't take up much water when the plant's foliage is not being stimulated by light. This means the roots will be sitting in a bog through the night and this can lead to root rot. Fortunately, I have not yet experienced this disaster although I've often irrigated at dusk.

When the air temperature inside drops down below 70°, which usually happens with the advent of winter, night watering should be suspended since there is some risk of the plant being overly chilled and, if it's near a window in winter, even frozen. Other than taking this precaution, I've watered morning and night with no ill effects.

Here are some additional tips on watering which should be helpful.

1. Water most plants less often in winter than in spring and summer. *Why?* Because most plants are semi-dormant in winter. The days are short, skies are overcast cutting down on light intensities, and the air is chilly. There is so little light striking the foliage and, hence stimulating growth that very little water is needed by the plant to "hold its own." In winter, give your plants just enough water to keep them alive. *Exceptions:* Some plants enter a period of growth in winter. Obviously, these should be given an adequate volume of water to fill their requirements.

2. Plants in sunny or partially-sunny locations, and even bright situations, need water more frequently than those living in less intense light level locations. *Why?* Because the high intensities of the light cause the plant to draw up more moisture from the soil and the heat causes the plant to transpire (throw off water vapor) at an accelerated rate. Another obvious reason is that heat dries out the soil rapidly. *Exceptions:* Cacti and other succulents usually don't need extra water in high light/heat environments because this is their natural habitat. Their succulent (water-storing) capacities carry them along quite nicely for many days.

3. Plants that are pot-bound need water more often than those which aren't. *Why?* Because a pot-bound plant's roots are so crowded and matted they are prevented from working efficiently and the plant needs considerably more moisture than other plants to support the heavier top growth that is typical of pot-bound specimens.

Misting and humidity. If your pores were obstructed so your skin couldn't "breathe", you'd soon expire. The same is true of plants. They have pores (stomata), too, and when these are clogged with dust, the plant can't carry on respiration and slowly suffocates. You can remedy this by washing the leaves monthly with a damp cloth or paper towel dipped in a lukewarm Ivory soap solution. The solution may be weak or strong, since Ivory has none of the caustic ingredients found in many other soaps or detergents. Follow with a clear-water rinse.

You should also invest in a hand squeeze-type atomizer which you can find at the five-and-dime or nursery for under two dollars. Get one with an adjustable nozzle which permits you to produce either a fine mist or a jet spray. Regular misting, to a limited degree, provide plants with the humidity they need to thrive. Plants growing in their natural habitat get this from rain and moisture condensation from the air. The air in most apartments and homes is really pretty wretched for any living thing—plant or man. It's hot, dry and stale most of the time and, in winter, all of the time. Plants (and people, too) need continually circulating fresh air, but fortunately for us, they settle for less. This is why raising the humidity around your plants, a minimum of once a week, preferably daily, assures their continued good health, all other things being equal.

If your collection is not too heavy or extensive, the best place to mist is in your bathtub or shower stall. Use a fine spray adjustment on the showerhead, select a lukewarm (never hot or cold) temperature, turn the water on low, and close the shower door. After a few minutes, turn the water off but let the plants continue to bask in the warm humid air for at least an hour.

The "heavyweights" obviously call for a less strenuous method. For a few dollars, you can purchase a vaporizer which raises the humidity by increasing the moisture in the air. This is most effective if the room is not overly large, but you can maintain the vaporizer's effectiveness in a large space by moving it directly under the plants. There are more elaborate and expensive mechanical devices and humidifiers which automatically maintain a selected humidity level. They range in price from a few dollars to several hundred dollars.

An alternative method, more primitive but just about as beneficial, is to use your hand mister. First of all, spread triple thicknesses of newspapers around the plant as far out as the "drip line" of the foliage. Make sure any nearby wood floors or furniture which might water spot are also covered, since airborne mist carries further than you might think, especially if there's a breeze wafting through the room. Then, starting at the top with your atomizer, work your way down, thoroughly saturating the top and undersides of the foliage. Within an hour, most of the water droplets will have evaporated and you can remove the newspapers.

Misting can sometimes be used as a substitute for watering. If a plant is flagging from the heat, for example, but you just watered two days ago, misting will often perk up the foliage. Newly-potted plants should always be misted as part of the initial watering process.

Brown, brittle leaf tips and edges are usually the result of inadequate humidity. One good method of raising the humidity around a plant for a longer period than misting achieves is to provide a microclimate by using water-covered pebbles in a tray or saucer under a plant. Simply defined, a microclimate is "a climate within a climate." The saucer or tray should extend beyond the base of the pot several inches. Pebbles or rocks—or even a block of wood—raise the base of the pot above the water level to avoid root rot. Over the next few days, the foliage is bathed in the rising waves of moist air. This process, on a small scale, duplicates what occurs when plants are growing naturally outdoors.

Your grandmother and her mother knew the beneficial effects of high humidity on plants and that the best-looking plants in the house were usually the ones grown in the kitchen and bathroom, where they frequently got a good steambath from the cooking and bathing activites of the family. Another yesteryear technique for raising humidity that's just as valid today is to put pans of hot water under your plants and let the steam rise under their foliage.

Chapter 4

Dormancy

Like most living things, plants require a period of rest, a respite from activity, a time to rejuvenate. In their natural habitat, cooling temperatures and diminishing daylight hours herald fall, the time when nature girds herself against the harshness of winter and begins conserving energy for the rigors of spring growth. It's the time when deciduous trees shed their leaves and cease taking nourishment. Houseplants, too, need a period of inactivity, and this is called *dormancy*.

If you are observant, you will be able to recognize the signs of natural dormancy when they occur. A plant that hasn't budged, so to speak, for a couple of weeks bears watching. You may have noted, for example, the beginnings of new foliage growth several days ago, but no further development. This is a pretty good indication that the plant has lapsed into dormancy. Withhold water and fertilizer from that point on and move the plant to a cool, dimly-illuminated corner until it "breaks" (which is the botanical term for resumption of growth).

Because of the unnatural environment in which houseplants exist, dormancy doesn't necessarily coincide with seasonal cycles, although the advent of shorter days and cooler air temperature often does trigger the phenomenon. Some plants may have more than one dormant period at anytime during the year, others you may have to force into dormancy, much as you would compel a hyperactive child to take his afternoon nap.

Forcing dormancy upon a plant which doesn't want to rest is usually easier and less demanding than forcing sleep on your intransigent offspring. Move the plant to a cool, dark place (cellar, closet, cabinet under the sink), away from windows and incandescent lights, and suspend food and water. (Fertilizer should be withheld through the winter months, as a matter of course.) The plant should react after a few days of this "solitary confinement" by sharply curtailing new growth and, perhaps, taking on a woebegone appearance.

When you notice the first sign of foliage activity, probably four to six weeks later, you may restore the plant to its former location. Water should be given in ever increasing amounts over the next few weeks, until you've reached the normal volume . . . a cup this week, a cup-and-a-half next week, and so on. The plant should perk up soon after and achieve even greater heights of horticultural splendor.

Never transplant during dormancy. The feeder roots are almost totally inactive and will not penetrate into the new soil. Both water and fertilizer are withheld during dormancy, but you need both when you repot, so the odds against potting a dormant specimen successfully are extremely high.

Chapter 5

Soil And Soil Amendments

There is as much controversy over what constitutes an ideal soil composition for houseplants among amateur and professional horticulturalists as there is over what is the best fertilizer, or water, or humidity level. At the risk of incurring the wrath of one quarter or another, I have found over the years that plants grow admirably in almost any soil formula. Of course, they do much better in a soil recipe which has been tailored to their individual preferences, but survive they will in just about any planting medium.

Soil from the garden or woods. I'm frequently asked if garden loam and rich topsoil from the woods are suitable for gardening. The answer is yes—for outdoor gardening. *Au naturel* soil can be very rich in nutrients. Trees, plants and flowers may flourish in it, but you run into problems when you try to use it as a potting medium for houseplants. First of all, it's usually full of grass and weed seeds which would rapidly crowd out anything else you tried to grow. It's also a safe bet that it's infested with larvae, grubs and insects which would make a feast of your prized specimens. Finally, with garden soil in particular, there is the danger that it is loaded with harsh fertilizers which are much too strong for the delicate systems of most houseplants.

The only time I might use soil from the garden or yard is if I were transferring a plant from the ground to a container. Even then, I would remove as much of the native soil as I could without damaging the plant's root system and replace it when I potted up with a good pasteurized soil mix.

There is a way you can make soil from the garden and woods relatively safe to use, if you have no easy access to packaged soil and you're willing to go to the trouble. It involves baking small quantities in your oven. Line a pan with aluminum foil or make a suitable container from heavy-duty foil, pour in a two-inch-deep layer of soil, mix in two cups of water, then bake for an hour at 215° to 225°. Stick pretty closely to these time/temperature recommendations. If you overdo it, microorganisms that improve soil fertility may be killed along with the pests and seeds. If it's done properly, the baking process actually enhances the fertility of the soil.

There is a minor odor problem with baking soil in an open pan. If you feel this would be bothersome, use a turkey-size "brown-in" bag, add one cup of water, seal, place the bag on a cookie sheet and bake an additional fifteen minutes.

Be sure to add the water. Dry-baked soil comes out like fine powder and is virtually impossible to handle.

The baking process gives you *pasteurized*, not *sterilized*, soil. Commercially-packaged soils are likewise pasteurized (or should be). To speak of sterilized soil in gardening is a misnomer. If the soil were truly sterilized, not much would grow in it.

What constitutes a good soil for houseplants? Hardly any of the commercially-prepared planting mixes are really "ready-to-use," as the package claims, but they're a good place to start. A problem which almost all packaged soil mixes share is lack of "body." Most are either superfine in texture, and consistent overhead watering packs them down into hardpan, or they are almost totally vermiculite or perlite, and very little soil. Commercially put-up soils are also usually devoid of two major ingredients conducive to trouble-free gardening—(1) bits of bark, wood or other bulky matter to give a plant's roots something stable to "grab" onto, and (2) coarse sand or gravel to hold the soil open and promote fast drainage of excess water.

There are some commercial mixes formulated for a particular horticultural use that are acceptable for use right from the package. Two which come to mind are "African Violet mix" and "Orchid mix." Both have the specialized ingredients these species require. A third commonly-available custom mix which I feel doesn't measure up is a national brand of "Cactus mix." It is far too light and contains little if any sand or appropriate substitute. If you intend growing a cactus garden, my recommendation is that you mix your own planting medium.

In addition to nutrient and mineral fortification, a good all-purpose planting mix should have pasteurized soil (to eliminate weed seeds and pest eggs), peat moss or a comparable substitute (for water absorbtion), leaf mold (for nutrients and to give the soil body), sand or gravel (for fast, efficient drainage of excess water), and a final ingredient which I favor—some horticultural charcoal (to "sweeten" the soil and neutralize the effects of decay and plant tissue breakdown). These additional ingredients are all soil *amendments*.

Soil amendments. Anything you put into soil that changes its basic character is an amendment. To amend is to change. Most soils need amending to create an optimum planting medium. Most potting soils, as we've seen, are so fine they need amendments to improve their ability to hold moisture and to admit air for the plant's root system to utilize.

You may use either *organic* amendments, which eventually decompose in the soil, or *mineral* amendments, which remain unchanged in the soil for decades. The former include such things as leaf mold, manure, peat moss, sphagnum moss, ground bark and sawdust; the latter, perlite, vermiculite, pumice and sand.

If you have no objection to their appearance, vermiculite and perlite are excellent amendments that improve a soil's moisture-holding capacity. Vermiculite, a mineral mica, is grey. Perlite, a porous rock of volcanic origin, is white. Both stand out noticeably in contrast to the soil in a pot, but this can be avoided by eliminating them in the last layer when you pot up.

Acid soils. A great many indoor plants thrive in a soil that is acid or partially acid. The acidity ("sourness") or alkalinity ("sweetness") of the soil is measured by the pH scale (hydrogen ion concentration) which runs from one to fourteen. If a soil has a pH factor of seven, for example, it is neutral and means it's evenly balanced between acidity and alkalinity. Anything below seven is acid; anything above is alkaline. Soils that have a lot of peat moss, oak or pine leaf mold or rotted hardwood sawdust are acid soils.

Following are some "ready-to-plant" soil formulations which you can mix yourself.

Basic Soil Recipe
(General Purpose Use)

3 parts pasteurized soil
1 part leaf mold
1 cup coarse builder's sand or gravel to each gallon of soil
½ cup of horticultural charcoal
2 tablespoons of steamed (not raw) bonemeal in the bottom layer of soil in the pot

To the above, you can add either vermiculite or perlite, about one cup to a gallon of soil, or one cup of shredded and soaked peat moss.

Acid Soil Recipe

5 parts shredded (and soaked) peat moss
2 parts oak leaf mold
1 part pasteurized soil
1 cup coarse builder's sand or gravel to each gallon of soil

½ cup of horticultural
charcoal
2 tablespoons of
steamed bonemeal
in bottom layer of
soil in pot

Again, you may add perlite or vermiculite in the same proportion as for a basic mix.

Fast-Draining Soil Recipe

Desert-type cacti
1 part coarse builder's sand
or gravel
1 part sandy soil
1 part limestone

Other succulents
1 part coarse builder's sand
or gravel
1 part shredded (and soaked)
peat moss, or 1 part ground
bark
1 part pasteurized soil
1 to 2 tablespoons of steamed
bonemeal in bottom layer of
soil in pot

Soil condition. Plants are surprisingly difficult to kill by ineptness, of even the grossest kind. They are forgiving to a fault. No matter what we do to them, they valiantly struggle to survive, and usually succeed. Some varieties even adapt, after a time, to daily drenching, when they normally require water only every ten days or so. Others adjust to either virtual darkness or to direct sun through a west window, when they probably prefer medium light.

Because plants are so amazingly adaptable, they'll usually tough it out regardless of the character of the soil, with the possible exception of continually wet conditions. This means that, if the soil in your pots doesn't measure up to the ideal mix, you shouldn't panic and repot all your specimens. If they are growing well, or more to the point, to your satisfaction, don't worry about soil problems. It is only when your plants begin to deteriorate that you should review or drasti-

cally alter your gardening procedures.

Ideally, though, your planting mix should contain the ingredients listed in the previous section. In addition, the soil should always be *friable*, which is a horticultural term that means "crumbly"—incapable of being packed together firmly into a ball.

Topsoil (about the first half-inch to inch) should periodically (once or twice a year) be replaced with fresh soil because overhead watering soon depletes almost all nutrients in the topsoil. Plants that are not too unwieldly should be knocked out annually to check both the condition of the soil and the roots. If the soil has traces of grey or white running through it, or is a hardpacked ball, replace it. If not, slip the pot back on and tap the base on a table top to reset the plant firmly in its pot.

Ultimately, most of the soil of a potted specimen will have to be replaced. If a plant has been growing for five years or longer in a pot, the soil is probably in a deplorable state. In all likelihood, it has absorbed a potentially dangerous amount of undissolved mineral salts (unused fertilizer) and continuous overhead watering week in and week out over the years has packed it down into hardpan—a term used to describe soil whose particles are so closely packed together that nothing —water, air or roots—can penetrate it easily. If the soil in your pots is rock-hard and crusty, and water takes forever to be absorbed, this is a classic case of hardpan and it's time to replace the soil with a fresh, virgin mix.

Replacing tired, old soil is a simple operation, but you have to be gentle. First of all, immerse the pot in a bucket, sink or tub of tepid water to which you've added a transplant shock preventive such as Vitamin B-1 or "Superthrive," for at least an hour. This should saturate the soil ball thoroughly and you need the soil very wet to remove it safely from the root system. You can't achieve this by overhead watering—you've got to dunk the pot.

Next, remove the pot and let the excess

drain for a few minutes, then knock out the plant as described in the chapter on potting. Any soil areas that look dry should be moistened. Working from the bottom, gently break away the clods of soil by rolling them gingerly between your thumb and fingers. The soil should crumble away from the roots easily.

Continue to work upward until most of the root system is exposed. Always leave some soil around the main root which is always dead center and is the root from which most of the foliage grows.

After cleaning the old pot (or use a fresh one), pour in a base layer of soil, then spread the roots out and begin to refill the pot with new soil, pressing it around the exposed roots gently but firmly. Continue this until you've reached the original soil line on the stem. Now water thoroughly and sit back. You'll probably see some depressions appear where the soil has settled. Firm in more soil and water again. Then, pick up the pot and, with your thumbs resting against the stem of the plant to steady it, slam the base of the pot against a wooden counter or table top. This will "set" the plant and cause soil to fall into any air pockets that may exist. Water again and refill the depressions, if they reappear.

You may have to stake the plant for a while, until the roots have anchored themselves in the new soil. Set the plant aside for about two weeks. Withhold food and water so that the roots can recover from the shock. Then, treat the plant as before.

Chapter 6

Fertilizers, Vitamins And Hormones

Fertilizer, or plant food, is highly-overrated in the cultivation of houseplants. Most beginners are easily persuaded by well-meaning friends and relatives that the secret of growing fat-and-sassy plants is to ply them with a steady flow of high-nitrogen goodies. Eventually, plants do need some nutritional help. Since they're trapped in the confines of their pots, they can't send their roots out on foraging expeditions to collect food. I said "eventually" because you don't have to worry about fertilizer for at least six months after you've bought a plant. The commercial grower has added more than enough to carry the plant for half a year. This is the reason for the recommendation in Chapter 1 that you flush out the excess fertilizer as soon as you get a new plant home.

Heavy feeding is not the answer to achieving an abundance of healthy foliage; in fact, the opposite is true. Consistent over-fertilizing will defoliate a plant and, quite possibly, kill it. Part of the fault for perpetuating this heavy-feeding-leads-to-bigger-and-better-plants myth lies with a few greedy retailers who are so dollar-conscious they'll push any product on the uninitiated. These are the same ones who never seem to have a small bottle or container of anything. It's always the "giant economy size" or a "two-year supply," when all you want is a one-shot dose. You end up, after a few years, with a garage crammed to the rafters with nearly-full bottles of chemicals which you'd never use in two lifetimes.

The blame must be shared by well-intentioned but uninformed novices who have been slowly murdering their own plants with everything from tea and lemon juice to cow manure and urea.

What to feed. There are organic and chemical fertilizers. The organics include such things as bonemeal, blood meal and cottonseed meal, and are usually high in only one of the three essential food elements. Chemical fertilizers are generally complete fertiliz-

ers—those which contain all three major food elements: nitrogen, phosphorous and potassium. These are almost always indicated on labels by their chemical symbols: N (nitrogen), P (phosphorous, or phosphate), K (potassium or potash), or numbers are used to indicate relative strength, such as 10-5-5, meaning 10 parts nitrogen to five parts each of phosphorus and potassium.

For general feeding, a complete fertilizer is preferable, and once you understand what various elements contribute to plant nutrition and health, you'll understand why. Nitrogen is of great importance since it is largely responsible for leaf development and plant growth. A plant that is deficient in nitrogen is usually stunted and the foliage yellows and drops off. But too much nitrogen can "burn" a plant's roots. If you want to nourish a plant fast, you'll need a brand which has nitrogen in nitrate (not nitrite) form. If you want a slower response, you should get a fertilizer with nitrogen in the ammonia form, listed on the label as ammonia nitrate.

Phosphorous, or phosphate, helps promote extensive root development, provides energy and causes a plant to mature faster. Potassium, or potash, also helps in root development and strengthens stems.

Another myth about fertilizers which needs exploding is that cow *manure* is the best of all fertilizers for houseplants and outdoor gardens. Most manures, depending upon the animal's diet, are very low in NPK (nitrogen, phosphorus, potassium) content, usually in the proportion 1-1-1. Manure is excellent, however, as a soil amendment and also contains some trace elements (small amounts of minerals) which are beneficial to plant growth.

Before you go skulking around the countryside collecting "chips" you should know that manure is available very reasonably from your nursery in deodorized and treated (to remove grass seeds) form. I would definitely advise against putting natural manure, direct from the beast, into your houseplant soil. If you've ever been downwind of a dairy farm, you'll immediately recognize the odor. On a warm day, your entire house will be, to quote Shakespeare, "The rankest compound of villainous smells that ever offended a nostril."

I find even deodorized manure hard to take. I once potted up some specimens using "odor-free" steer manure as a soil amendment. Although it was purportedly deodorized, after the initial watering I detected a faint trace of Eau de Barnyard. When I noticed guests who were seated near the offending plants surreptitiously sniffing the air, then listing strangely to one side, I knew it was time to knock out the plants and slightly alter their soil recipe. I'm sure those guests (who never returned incidentally) are still wondering what I was doing to my plants to create such an offensive odor, and are convinced that no one who wasn't a bit weird could live with it. Perhaps, this belated explanation will vindicate me.

One of the safest of all fertilizers, and the one most often recommended for novice gardeners, is *bonemeal* (steamed, not raw). It is an organic compound and breaks down slowly, releasing nutrients and trace elements (calcium, magnesium, sulphur, iron, manganese, boron, copper and zinc) for months. Because it contains no nitrogen, root burn is virtually impossible. Bonemeal should only be applied when you pot up. About two tablespoons sprinkled in the bottom layer of soil are adequate.

Another relatively-safe general-purpose plant food is fish emulsion. It, too, is organic, but is also a complete fertilizer. There is little danger of root burn, provided you follow the dilution directions or, better yet, if you dilute more than recommended. You can get either natural, which ranks with unprocessed manure for rustic bouquet, or deodorized fish emulsion. In either form, always check the label to make sure it has chelated iron. (A chelating agent releases an element "locked" in the soil and makes it immediately available to the plant.)

40

The use of fish as a plant food goes back centuries. Our Pilgrim ancestors were amazed to see American Indians putting a fish under each corn plant. Whether the practice came down to them from antiquity, or whether they stumbled on it, isn't known. (As things have turned out for the American Indians, they probably wish now that, instead of a fish, they had put a Pilgrim under each corn plant.)

Plants respond well to periodic changes in diet, so it's beneficial to alternate fish or whale emulsion with another type of food. Whatever you feed should be a complete fertilizer (remember, a complete fertilizer has nitrogen, phosphorous and potash).

What about vitamins and hormones? Once a month, through spring and summer, you can add a vitamin-hormone booster (such as "Superthrive") in the water you give your plants. This is in addition to, not in place of, your regular plant food program. Vitamins and hormones can't do the job of providing a balanced nutritional program for a plant, since they don't have the ingredients contained in a complete fertilizer.

Some indoor gardeners view their plants as garbage disposals. They pour tea, lemon juice and vinegar into their plants' pots, and more than a few put tomatoes, potato peelings and other leftover vegetables into a blender, add water, and churn up a mixture of glop which they proceed to give their plants. It's hard to comprehend why they would want to endanger their plants' well-being with these home-grown and antiquated nostrums when there are so many inexpensive, safe and tried-and-true additives available.

In your great-grandmother's day, a weak tea and an even weaker solution of water and vinegar were used as sources of acid for acid-loving specimens to green up chlorotic plants, but nothing else was available then. Today all that has changed. Still, all over the world, people are killing off hundreds of plants daily by pouring lemon juice, vinegar, and who knows what else into their plants.

Even though a plant that has been force-fed a dose of lemon juice or vinegar or what-have-you is apparently thriving, it is doing so in spite of the feeding, not because of it. If there were any real merit in these unconventional concoctions, commercial growers and arboretums would have been using them long ago. To my knowledge, none of them is.

How to feed. Always wet down the soil in the pot before you pour in fertilizer solutions. Unless the tiny root hairs are wet, there's a good chance that they'll suffer from nitrogen burn, which means they lose moisture and the tissue begins to deteriorate.

Most fertilizers that are manufactured and packaged for interior use are made to be diluted in water and applied to the soil. Some are dry, in powder or tablet form; most are liquid and these are the easiest to use. While I generally recommend following label directions to the letter, when it comes to fertilizers, I lean toward the school of thought which teaches it is better to give a weaker solution more frequently than the stronger, label-directed feeding less often. After all, this is how plants normally feed in their natural habitat.

For example, the label direction on a popular brand fish emulsion fertilizer says: "Feed established plants in pots and planters one ounce (2 tablespoons) per gallon of water once a month." I dilute an ounce in *two* gallons and feed *twice* a month, suspending all feeding during the winter months and dormancy.

When to feed. Ninety-five percent of the plants we grow indoors enter their vigorous growth period in spring and continue to throw out new foliage until fall, pretty much the same as plants growing outdoors. As the air cools and the days grow shorter and duller, root activity and foliage production slow and may even come to a brief halt as a plant enters dormancy.

It should be obvious that a plant needs more of everything when it's active and thriving, and less or nothing when it's inactive and resting. This long prelude is leading up to this: Withhold all fertilizer from traditional foliage plants from about October through March. As we've seen, a plant has no need for food when it's on vacation. If you persist in feeding it year round, it will soon begin to deteriorate and, finally, give up.

What about those convenient little tablets —those innocent-looking plant food pellets which come in the foil packet? If you are an inexperienced gardener, give a wide berth to these highly-touted but potentially deadly pills. These are the ones you stick under the topsoil, where they're supposed to dissolve slowly over a period of days or weeks. The theory behind them is sound: As they dissolve, the nutrients are diluted by the water and give a plant a regulated supply of food, rather than a sudden dose. I've tried several different brands to give them a fair shake and, in the majority of cases, found that the pellets either obstinately refused to dissolve, even after weeks, or that they disintegrated too rapidly, loading the soil with a very dangerous concentration of nitrogen.

Foliar feeding. Thanks, in large measure, to the pioneering work of Cornell University's Dr. Harold Tukey, Jr., we now know that nutrients applied to the foliage can be absorbed and utilized rapidly by a plant to correct a deficiency or improve its condition. Within a few minutes, the leaves begin to absorb the nutrients and continue to do so for up to two days.

Foliar feeding is especially useful as a "booster shot" to newly-potted specimens and particularly air layered cuttings which have only minimal root structure. Until a plant has developed new feeder roots, it must tap its resources of stored nutrients to sustain life. If these reserves are depleted before the feeder roots have formed, the plant may not survive. Foliar feeding provides the necessary nutrition to carry the plant through this critical period.

Foliar feeding shouldn't replace soil fertilization though. The dilution called for when you use foliar sprays is so weak, and the length of effectiveness so short, you must periodically feed via the soil to keep the plant lush and green.

Chapter 7

Is There A Doctor In The House?

You must accept the fact that your plants may not always be picture-perfect, vigorous and healthy. Even with the best of care, a plant can suddenly develop problems. It may be nothing more serious than an iron deficiency, which can be easily remedied, or something major, such as an invasion of parasitic insects, which calls for drastic action and long-term observation.

Because plants have no built-in natural defenses and are vulnerable to attack from several quarters, we must be aware of their disorders and responsive to their needs.

Avoidable Disorders

First of all, let's take the problems which *we* inflict on our plants through a lack of understanding of their needs, in most cases, but through obstinacy and indifference (tsk! tsk!), in a few instances.

Sunburn is easy to diagnose. If a plant has been sitting in direct sun and develops circular brown spots the size of a quarter or larger on its leaves, the plant is sunburned. This is a frequent plant disorder because some people just will not accept the fact that houseplants, conditioned to the low-light levels of our homes, can't take being set outside for a sunbath. Most houseplants have never seen direct sun, having lived a sheltered life in the protection of the greenhouse. Putting them outside for even a few minutes in direct sun, or even in a window that gets unobstructed sun, is the kiss of death for most specimens. The least that will happen is a severe and noticeable burn; the worst is an untimely demise from heat prostration.

Remedy: A sunburned plant can be salvaged by moving it to a spot that gets no di-

rect sun or putting a thin curtain or shade between the plant and the window. Damaged leaves can be pruned off (but will never be replaced). Emergency first aid may be necessary in the form of deep watering with warm water and a thorough misting or wetting down of the foliage.

Some foliage plants, *Ficus benjamina* (weeping fig), for example, all desert cacti and many succulents, can take direct sun, if you provide good cross-ventilation so that the solar-heated air doesn't build up to dangerous levels around the plant.

Brown, brittle leaves. This condition is commonplace to some extent, and can result from more than one cause. (1) *Brown leaf tips* are almost always brought about by consistently-low humidity, as we've seen earlier. It may be comforting to know that nearly every indoor gardener, novice and expert alike (including myself), have brown leaf tips on some of their plants.

(2) *Browning off or brown spots along the edges* of leaves is often the result of overfeeding, especially with a high nitrogen fertilizer. The condition is sometimes called "salt injury" and this diagnosis is correct if the soil looks washed out and greyish and if the pot is tinged with white stains which are visible evidence of leeched-out salts.

(3) Overwatering is the cause if the *stem browns off*.

(4) *Wilting* of the foliage preceding browning off is the hallmark of dehydration, or insufficient moisture. In this case, the lower leaves are usually the first to go.

Remedies: (1) Raise the humidity around the plant by misting twice a day and/or use a microclimate, as described in Chapter 3. (2) Stop feeding the plant for at least three months. Try to flush the excess fertilizer out of the pot by heavy watering with tepid water. Scour off any white stains and algae that may be on the outside of the pot with hot water and steel wool or a wire-bristle brush. An extreme solution is to repot the plant in fresh soil. (3) First of all, let the soil dry out completely, which means a drought period of ten to fourteen days. This will give the plant's roots, which are probably also damaged, a chance to recover. Then, cut back on the frequency of irrigations, but not the volume of water you give the plant. Use the finger-in-the-soil technique to determine when it's time to give the plant a drink. (4) The opposite extreme is treating healthy foliage plants like cacti and withholding water until the plant's roots die of thirst. Again, use your finger to guide you. On the average, healthy, thriving plants need water about every seven to ten days.

Leaf loss is another problem which has several potential causes. One of the most frequent is (1) *root shock* when the plant was potted up. This usually affects the entire plant, not just the lower branches.

(2) Occasionally, a plant that seems "in the pink" will begin dropping leaves that are green and apparently healthy. Almost without exception, the culprit is *red spider mites* which have gone undetected.

(3) *Overwatering* figures into this problem, also—usually when the lower leaves are dropped first.

(4) A sudden, drastic *shift in temperature* can bring on the condition, again with the loss of lower leaves followed by wilting of the rest of the foliage.

Remedies: (1) Root shock is almost irreversible, but plants sometimes struggle back from death's door. Your best chance for salvaging a root-shocked plant is to knock it out, trim away some of the outside root structure and most of the foliage, repot it and give it a Vitamin B-1 booster (no fertilizer, however). Set the plant aside in a dim-to-medium light location with no water until you see some new, vigorous growth. (2) See the following section on plant pests for tips on coping with the insidious spider mites. (3) This one is obvious: Move the plant to a location where the temperature level remains fairly constant, day and night. It should recover but, of course, will never replace the lost foliage.

Plant Maladies

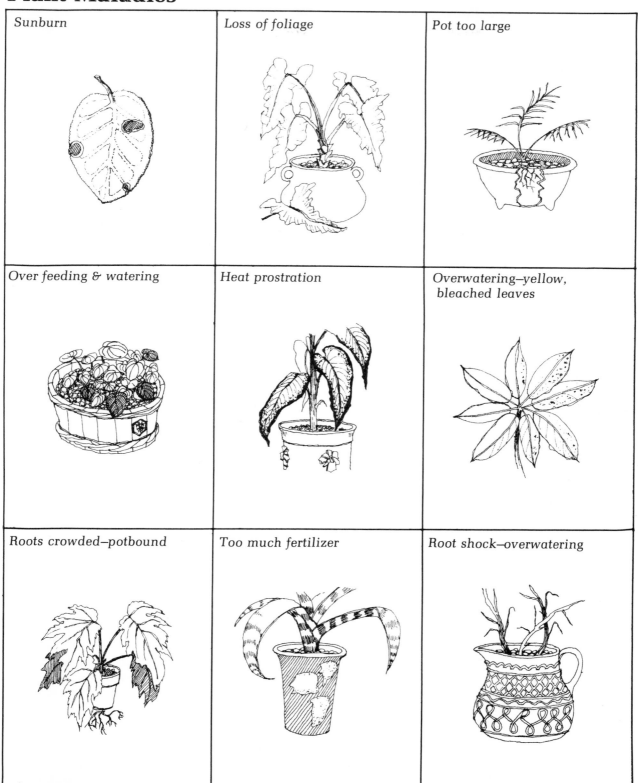

Sunburn	Loss of foliage	Pot too large
Over feeding & watering	Heat prostration	Overwatering—yellow, bleached leaves
Roots crowded—potbound	Too much fertilizer	Root shock—overwatering

Yellowing of the foliage, or chlorosis, is symptomatic of an insufficiency of chlorophyll (green coloring matter) in a plant and is usually the result of inadequate chelated iron in the soil. The correct diagnosis is chlorosis if foliage throughout the plant is affected by the symptom of overall yellowing, with the exception of leaf veins, which remain green. Yellowing and eventual loss of lower leaves is a natural phenomenon as the plant matures. Lower leaves are generally sacrificed in favor of new top growth.

Remedy: Either give the plant a chelated iron additive or a fertilizer high in chelated iron content. The iron must be chelated (KEE'late·ed), which means it is immediately available to the plant. Otherwise, the plant would have to wait months for natural breakdown and absorbtion process to take place.

Pale, widely-spaced leaves are always the result when a plant is not getting sufficient light. The paling (technically, *etiolation*) comes from insufficient chlorophyll production. A plant needs good light to produce chlorophyll.

Remedy: Move the plant closer to a natural light source, or supplement natural light with artificial illumination.

General, sudden collapse. Another condition brought on by any one of several causes is total collapse of a plant, in which the foliage suddenly wilts and sags.

(1) *Heat prostration* could be the villain. When the interior temperature rises above 80°, especially if the shift was rapid, as during a heatwave, a plant can't carry on transpiration successfully.

(2) *Root shock* is sometimes responsible if a plant's roots were traumatized during potting.

(3) *Dehydration* can also bring it on, especially during hot, summer "dog days."

(4) Finally, a long-term *pot-bound* condition may finally catch up with the plant.

Remedies: (1) Raise the humidity, as previously discussed, and provide cross ventilation. If you can't open windows to achieve this, use a small fan to cool down the air and to keep it circulating. (2) Unfortunately, as we've seen, there isn't a great deal you can do to treat root shock, other than the root-foliage trimming and the Vitamin B-1 booster previously recommended. (3) Deep watering and frequent misting will sometimes rejuvenate a flagging plant. (4) If a plant has suffered for a long time with a chronic root-bound condition before "throwing in the sponge," it's probably too late to save it. If you're willing to take a chance on losing it, for sure, in order to attempt rescue, you may want to consider this drastic operation. It has worked for me more often than not, but I only use it when there is no alternative. Knock out the plant, lay it's root ball on a firm surface, take a sharp knife and make four or five vertical slashes into the root system, rotating the plant as you cut. Trim off some of the top growth to give the roots a rest. Then repot conventionally (using a new pot two inches larger) and water with a Vitamin B-1 solution or "Superthrive." Then, set the plant aside in dim light for at least two weeks without any food or water. When (and if) you see new growth budding, you were successful and you can treat the plant normally again.

What occurs when you slash the roots is massive trauma. If the plant is still struggling to survive, the shock often stimulates the development of new roots and this activity revives the plant. In effect, it saves itself.

Now, some words of caution. Sterilize the knife that you intend to use with a fungicide or antiseptic solution, and this is particularly important if you've used the knife in previous horticultural operations without cleaning it. Also, the only time you should attempt this surgery is in spring or summer—the peak of the growing season—which enhances your chances for success.

Fungus diseases. Most fungi and related problems are the result of overly moist soil and stagnant air. Fungus disease, mold and mildew almost never occur in a collection when the area they're grown in receives periodic changes of fresh air, even though the topsoil is damp most of the time.

(1) *Leaf spot* or *leaf blight* is probably the most common fungus disease, producing white or pale patches on leaves and soft brown spots on stems. You may also see black areas in the spots, which are the fruiting bodies of the fungus.

(2) *Powdery mildew* is more commonly found outdoors but, if the conditions are right (high humidity and stagnant air) it can strike indoors. The symptoms are gray or white powder on leaves and stem. The affected areas may dry out and shrivel.

(3) *Crown rot* is another disorder which seldom plagues the indoor gardener, but it does strike occasionally. The fungus, *Scleratium delphinii*, causes the plant's crown to rot and topple.

(4) *Root rot* results from overwatering and can be caused by several similar fungi.

Remedies: (1) Prune away and discard affected foliage (don't let it fall and remain on healthy foliage or on the topsoil which would spread the fungus). Treat the foliage and stem with sulphur dust, which is available at most nurseries and plant shops. Provide better ventilation and, if this isn't feasible, use a small fan to keep the air moving continuously around the plant. (2) Dusting with sulphur may clear up the condition and better air circulation prevents its occurrence. (3) No known remedy. Plants afflicted with crown rot should be discarded. Replacement plants should be given better air circulation from the outset. (4) Ninety percent of the plants affected by root rot are beyond redemption and should be tossed. Terra cotta pots should be sterilized before using again by immersing them in boiling water for at least five minutes. Plastic pots should be washed in a strong detergent, then treated with a fungicide. In the future, your watering can should be less active.

Springtails and fungus gnats are two common annoyances which usually appear in spring and summer, when your plants are watered more often and the topsoil is wet or damp most of the time. The wet topsoil is the key. The appearance of both is always preceded and precipitated by continually damp soil. Springtails can damage seedlings, but there is no evidence that either can damage established plants. Springtails are the tiny white critters which move rapidly across the topsoil. The gnats fly more or less constantly around the host plant. Allowing the soil to dry out eliminates both.

Plant Parasites

Since houseplants are exposed to the outdoors for only brief periods, there is little danger of attack from the hundreds of insects which plague outdoor gardeners. We have only a few pests to contend with and, usually, these destructive parasites were in the soil or hidden on the foliage and stem, sometimes as minute eggs, when the plant was acquired.

No matter how closely a specimen is examined before purchase, soil-borne infestation and predator eggs are virtually impossible to detect. This is why you are cautioned to isolate a new plant and keep an eye on it for three or four weeks, before you introduce it to your other plants.

Our first thought, when we discover unwelcome company has moved in with our plants, is "Death to the Infidels!" or something equally ferocious. This is the appropriate reaction, but there is a natural tendency for us to overdo. So, before we take a look at houseplant parasites and how to deal with them, let's explore some of the potential dangers of overkill and the excessive use of lethal, long-lasting pesticides.

Pesticide dangers. In the years before we were knowledgeable about the long-term effects that many insecticides have on our environment, deadly sprays were employed indiscriminately in the control and prevention of insects and plant disease. Today, we are paying the price. We now know the tragic consequences of our unbridled use of the most pernicious of all pesticides, DDT. Entire species of wildlife (the pelican, for example) are on the verge of extinction because of the cumulative effects of DDT in their systems. We have also upset the balance of nature by eliminating many beneficial insects—natural enemies of the destructive species.

We humans, too, are carrying around concentrations of DDT in our bodies. It is often found even in the milk our children drink. Medical science has not yet determined the potential danger this poses to generations yet unborn or, more immediately, to our future well-being.

It is difficult to comprehend, in the face of overwhelming evidence of the catastrophic effects of DDT, why it is still being widely used. Even some of the nation's most prestigious arboretums, which should be four-square against this insidious insecticide, are still routinely using DDT in their pest control programs.

A large share of the responsibility for the proliferation of pesticides which are decimating wildlife and disrupting the ecological balance of our planet must be borne by the chemical companies who, like irresponsible land developers, put the dollar ahead of all else. Their business is based on developing deadlier, longer-lasting pesticides, then promoting their universal use by heavily funded advertising programs.

Pesticide manufacturers' favorite argument is that the world's current high crop yields would be impossible without effective control of insect invaders. This is unquestionably true; but, most of us who are concerned about what's happening to our wildlife feel it is incumbent upon the pesticide manufacturers to spend some of their huge profits on research and development of insecticides that are harmless to humans, birds, fish and other wildlife, and are degradable in the soil.

The alternative to the use of pesticides is organic gardening, in which natural enemies of destructive insects and organic compounds are employed. Admittedly, the re-sults are usually not as impressive (although this isn't always true) but, until science develops safe substitutes for the dangerous insecticides, we should be willing to accept something less than perfection.

Insect invaders and how to cope. Virtually all pests which attack houseplants are sucking insects. They damage or kill by tapping into the lifeline of sap and, vampire-like, drawing out a plant's vitality. These include scale, mealybugs, aphids and spider mites —the four common invaders.

The most effective, long-term solution to controlling sucking insects is the application of a systemic-type poison directly into the soil in the pot. Unlike insecticides which are sprayed, thereby creating a potential danger to wildlife and beneficial insects from drifting mist and build-up in the earth, the lethal effect is confined to the container.

A systemic poison is absorbed by the plant's roots and spreads throughout the stem and foliage system, hence the name. Insects which attempt to feed on a systemically-treated plant's sap are soon eliminated. The advantages of this method of control are legion: (1) Systemic poison has a residual effect and takes care of future invasions. (2) It is harmless to the plant. (3) It can be administered directly into the soil, so there is no danger of spray drift or inhalation of noxious fumes.

Three popular systemic pesticides are Cygon (or Dimenthoate), Di-syston, and Metasystox-R. These are organic phosphates which are highly toxic and should be treated with respect. Although it is possible, in some cases, to spray them, it is much safer ecologically and more effective to apply them to the soil.

Aphids (or plant lice.) These tiny invaders come in several colors—yellow, green, black, pink—but regardless of their color, the damage is just as severe. Because they extract sap from a plant, they can stunt or distort growth and, if permitted to colonize unchecked, can defoliate and finally kill their victim. Like

Plant Pests

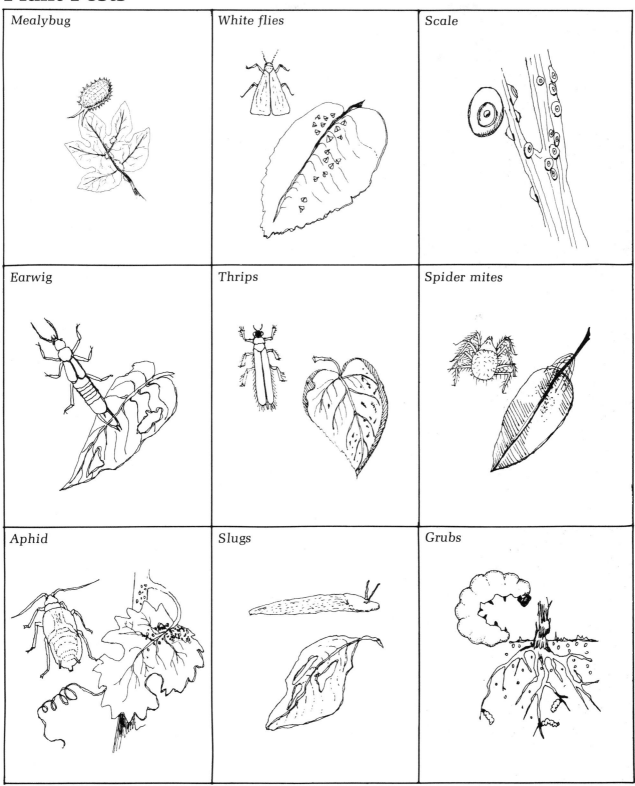

Mealybug

White flies

Scale

Earwig

Thrips

Spider mites

Aphid

Slugs

Grubs

49

Mealybugs can be removed with a cotton swab dipped lightly in alcohol.

scales, they excrete a tacky substance called honeydew that soon attracts ants. In fact, this sudden visitation of ant hordes is usually the first indication, for most unwary gardeners, that they have an aphid problem. Again, an Ivory soap solution and warm water generously applied to the foliage usually dislodges most aphids, but you may have to repeat the process in a few days.

• ORGANIC TREATMENT:

(1) Ladybugs are natural enemies of aphids. They'll "clean" an infested plant in no time. Many nurseries and plant shops are now stocking ladybugs for organic gardeners.

(2) Many aphids are soil-borne and some attack roots. Use "Bull Durham" tobacco as a mulch on the topsoil. Not only is it effective as a repellent, it also has plant food value.

• PESTICIDE TREATMENT: Since both Pyrethrum (py-REE′thrum) and Rotenone (RO′ten-own) are plant derivatives—Pyrethrum comes from chrysanthemums and Rotenone from the roots of the derris and cubé plants—they probably could be listed under the organic heading. But, since both are toxic to fish (but harmless to man and animals) it seems appropriate to list them as

pesticides. Follow label directions for dilution and application.

Mealybugs are easy to recognize and usually easier than most pests to eradicate. They look like tiny puffs of cotton and prefer to cluster in colonies under leaves and in stem joints, away from bright light. The safest method of treatment, without resorting to poisons and oils, is to use a cotton swab dipped in alcohol to remove them. Once you've found mealybugs on a plant, isolate it immediately and inspect it carefully every two or three days after treatment. Although the alcohol-swab treatment is effective for combating small invasions, it has no residual effect and you may have missed the minute mealybug eggs. Seriously infested plants, with deep, almost inaccessible crevices where mealybugs can thrive unmolested, should be discarded.

• ORGANIC TREATMENT: Mineral and vegetable oil compounds used as a spray.

• PESTICIDE TREATMENT: Application of a systemic poison in the soil.

Red Spider Mites are also sucking insects. The ravages of mite infestation cause yellow and reddish blotches on leaves with powdery webby undersides. Not all spider mites are red; they can be green, yellow or black. If you suspect that a plant has mites, there is a simple way to find out for sure. Hold a piece of white paper under the foliage, tap the leaves several times, then examine the paper in bright light. If you see tiny critters scampering about, your plant has mites. A treatment that is sometimes effective, if the infestation isn't too severe, is to hose off the plant with a gentle mist. You can even do this in the shower. Mites loathe moist, humid conditions, so frequent misting or hosing off (don't forget the undersides of leaves) is a good preventive control.

• ORGANIC TREATMENT:

(1) Mix wheat flour with buttermilk until you achieve a consistency that will spray. Thoroughly wet tops and undersides of

foliage and don't forget the stem. Repeat in two weeks, if needed.

(2) Lime-sulphur, summer or winter strength, whichever is appropriate.

(3) Potassium Sulphide (one ounce diluted in two gallons of water) is also an effective spray control.

• PESTICIDE TREATMENT: Application of a systemic poison to the soil.

Scales. Armored and unarmored scales are the primary types which attack indoor plants, showing a preference for ferns, palms and *Ficus decora* (rubber tree). They are insidious little beasties, marvelously protected by nature under a hard, armadillo-like shell which, to the untrained eye, appears to be a natural part of the plant. Scales do their damage by inserting their thread-like mouths into the leaf and stem and slowly extracting sap from the plant. You'll see the results of their activity in yellowing leaves, dead branches and stunted growth, and deposits of sticky honeydew on leaves and branches. Eventually, the entire plant dies if it is not treated. The best approach to control, though, are preventive measures. Annihilate the adolescents and break the cycle of infestation. Female scales give birth to their brood once a year, in the spring. The young crawl out from under their mother's shell and spread throughout the plant. This is the time to mount an offensive, before they have had a chance to form their own protective shell.

Armored scales have a hard, waxy, dull-brown shell (scale) over their bodies which protects them from almost any insecticide or predatory insect. *Unarmored* scales are un-armored in name only; they are usually larger and softer, but still are safely ensconced in a chitinous shell. Adult scales can be removed with a thumbnail or dull edge of a paring knife. For a more drastic solution, use a systemic poison.

• ORGANIC TREATMENT: Lime-sulphur, winter strength when the plant is dormant, summer strength during vigorous growth period.

• PESTICIDE TREATMENT: Nicotine sulfate solution or melathion (both relatively low in toxicity and hazards).

Some important footnotes. If you have small children around, or pets which are fond of chomping on plants or digging in the soil, don't use any poisonous substance in or on your plants. Most pesticides and insecticides are lethal if taken internally. Also, if you decide to ignore my advice against using "bug bombs," which is your perogative, be extremely careful not to inhale any of the spray mist. Never use a bug bomb indoors; that's really asking for it.

One of the safest methods of dealing with plant parasites, which is successful against everything but scales, is to wash down the foliage with Ivory bar soap suds and warm water, then thoroughly hose or syringe off the foliage with clear water. Soap will not harm plants, provided you keep it out of the soil by covering the top of the pot with aluminum foil and if you completely remove any residue by rinsing. Why not try this simple method before resorting to pesticides?

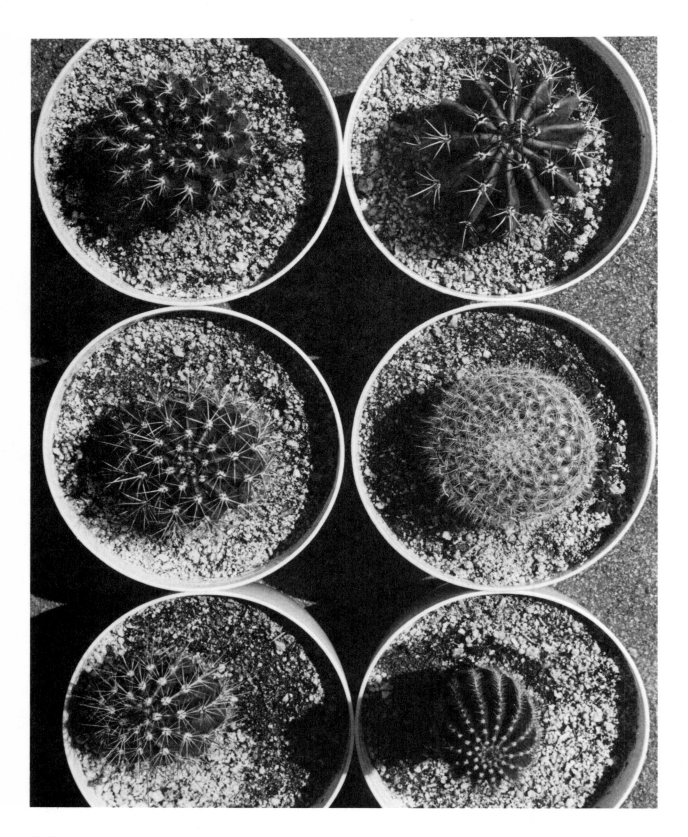

Chapter 8

Cacti And Other Succulents— The Water-less Plants

There is a whole different world of foliage and bloom for those who love greenery but whose environmental conditions or personal disposition make the culture of traditional foliage plants impractical or impossible. This is the cactus and succulent ("spineless cactus") universe. It offers unlimited potential for variety in size, shape, color, floral display, and other distinctive characteristics, while making few demands upon its caretaker.

The word *succulence* in botany means the ability to store water and the term *succulent* is given to about 7,000 species including some 2,000 species of cactus. Because the culture requirements of cacti (members of the botanical family *Cactaceae*) are somewhat different, they are usually automatically excluded when amateur horticulturalists discuss succulents, which are not as hardy as their thorny brothers. For the purposes of this discussion, we will do the same.

Succulents. Very few succulents come from the arid desert areas where evaporation exceeds rainfall. Most are native to the semi-desert regions where the sun is less intense and rainfall more frequent and abundant. Here are some of the most commonly-grown succulents:

Agave (uh-GAVE'vih) Native to the North and South American continents, members of the Agave family are usually huge plants in maturity and include the famous *A. americana*, or century plant, which was once believed to bloom only every 100 years. In recent years, it has been established that this specimen may bloom twice or three times each century. Probably the best species for indoor cultivation are *A. victoriae-reginae*, which has narrow, dark green leaves accented with white; *A. stricta*, and *A. filifera*.

Aloe (ALL'owe) Long a household favorite, these African natives are prized primarily for their striking foliage characteristics: soaring, jagged, spiked leaves. Flowers are red or orange and bell-shaped. Some varieties are sources for medicine and incense. Since they are winter-growers, they need less water in spring and summer.

Echeveria (etch-eh-vuh-REE'uh) Another popular succulent family, *Echeveria* produce green or grey-green leaves in rosettes. Some varieties are stemless, others have branching stems. Flowers are red or orange, but if you prefer large rosettes to floral output, remove any buds that appear.

Haworthia Native to Africa, this genus is a winter-grower and offers a wide variety of interesting species, many with small rosettes and white flowers held aloft in spike-like clusters.

Kalanchoe (kal-AN'koe-ee) Africa and Asia are continents of origin for this genus which includes plants previously classified as *Bryophyllum*. Probably the best known variety is the *K. pinnata* (also called air plant and life plant) which produces plantlets on its leaf edges and yellow flowers with reddish overtones. It must have more moisture than most succulents to thrive.

Sedum (SEE'dum) Indigenous to the Northern Hemisphere, varieties of this genus produce thick, compactly-set leaves on stalks. As the plant matures, new shoots develop at the base. The most often collected species is the delicate *S. Morganianum*, or Donkey's tail, which trails cords of plump foliage and looks best as a hanging plant. If abused or overwatered, it drops its leaves, but can be cut back and re-started. Broken leaves can be rooted again by sticking them back into the pot, but this soon becomes a nuisance.

Cacti offer great variety in size, shape, color, and floral display.

Sempervivum (sem-per-VYE'vum) species are characterized by thickly set rosettes of leaves. *S. tectorum* is the popular variety commonly known as "hen and chickens" because of the plant's habit of throwing tiny offsets around its base, calling to mind a mother hen herding her chicks.

Basic care for succulents *Soil.* A mix composed mainly of organic material and sharp builder's sand is ideal for succulents. Peat moss, ground bark, or leaf mold will serve as the organic ingredient. Steamed bonemeal in the bottom soil layer is beneficial. Succulents require fast-draining potting media. *Light.* Generally speaking, a bright, diffuse-light window location is best for succulents. A thin, filmy curtain should be between the window and the plant to minimize the harsh rays of the sun. To prove the adaptability of individual plants, I've kept some succulents, such as the *Crassula*, in windows which get direct sun for three hours a day without sunscorch. In fact, I have one now which survived without ill effects throughout the past summer in a west window which built up temperatures to 110°. It was necessary to water every four days to keep the leaves from wilting, but this was the only special care required. *Water.* Irrigate when the soil feels dry. Depending upon the environmental conditions in interior locations, this could be every week, ten days, or fortnight. *Temperature.* Most succulents prefer cooler conditions than other houseplants, but seem to take the normal household ranges in stride. In their natural habitat, they are exposed to summer daytime temperatures in excess of 120°, on occasion, and winter nighttime extremes which plummet near freezing. *Fertilizer.* When you pot up or pot on,

54

sprinkle a couple of tablespoons of steamed bonemeal in the bottom layer of soil. Once a year, at the peak of the plant's growing season, feeding with a complete fertilizer is beneficial. *Re-potting* is usually necessary only once every two or three years, particularly if the specimen is a fairly shallow-root species, such as the *Echeveria* and *Sempervivum*. *Propagation.* You can increase your stock from seeds, from cuttings of lateral branches which can be separated from the understock (stem), usually without detracting from the appearance of the donor plant, or from leaf cuttings. To pot up stem and leaf cuttings, allow them to cure for three or four days out of the sun so their cut ends can dry out and callus. Once the wound has healed, stick the cuttings in a potting medium (sand is a good root-starter) and leave them until roots have formed. When you're ready to pot up the cuttings, your soil mix must be dry. Fill about a quarter of the pot with crocking and the other three quarters with your mix. Set the roots gently on the surface of the soil and anchor the cutting in place, either by criss-crossing rubber bands over the top and around the base of the pot or by imbedding two label markers (like crutches) on either side of the cutting. A pinch or two of potting soil may be sprinkled over the roots, but you must never bury the fleshy base of the succulent or it will rot. No water yet! Set the newly-potted cutting aside in a bright sunless spot for a week, then mist or dribble a few droplets of water on the roots. Repeat every three or four days until about three weeks have passed. Then, you may water normally. Provided you've performed all operations correctly, the cutting should take root and eventually become a handsome specimen.

Cacti. Few people are neutral about cacti. Most either love them or can't abide the little porcupines. I fear I fall into the latter group. It's really difficult, for me at least, to entertain thoughts of adopting anything as menacing as these spiked and spiny denizens of the desert. I like to move around my plants, preening, pruning and tending to their needs. It's therapeutic for me as well as my plants. They need occasional flurries of attention. Cacti, on the other hand, neither require nor wish fussing over. If you overdo the T.L.C., they'll give you a painful sting for your efforts. They can get along without you very well—99% of the time.

The term cactus comes from the Greek word, *kaktos*, meaning "spiny plant," and most live up to their name. Some species have—instead of or in addition to, a mantle of thorns—downlike hairs. The spines probably evolved by cacti as biological necessities, to assure preservation of the species. Foraging animals in the arid and barren desert tracts would soon wipe out the cacti for their water reservoirs if it were not for these sharp punishing spikes. The fuzz and hair which shrouds some species is nature's buffer against the blistering desert sun which would otherwise literally dehydrate a cactus to death.

Most desert cacti have two things in common: (1) Most species require at least six hours of direct sun each day (more in the winter) to thrive and bloom, and (2) almost all do best in dry soil that drains fast and well. Other than providing these simple conditions, you can neglect cacti for months without risk of endangering their well-being. There are exceptions, such as the epiphytic jungle cacti, which will be discussed in the following description of popular cacti genera.

Desert cacti. *Chamaecereus silvestri*, commonly called the peanut cactus, is fairly compact and cylindrical in shape, with prostrate stems and well-developed spines. It produces red flowers two to three inches long from about April through July. Hybrid members throw blooms of pastel hues in reds, pinks, oranges and yellows.

Corypantha elephantidens and *C. vivipara.* Cylindrical in shape, they may grow as a single plant or in clumps. Both are recognizable by the pronounced depression which appears on the upper side of each tubercle. *C. elephantidens* is the larger of the two. *C. vivipara* produces purple flowers.

Enchinopsis. Popularly named the sea urchin and hedgehog cactus, there are many varieties from which to choose, as a result of continuing hybridization, and all are easy to grow. Most species are small and somewhat globular with straight ribs. If fertilized, they produce flowers with long tubes in shades of yellow, pink, red, and white in summer. They throw offsets readily and these should be removed for more abundant flowering.

Ferocactus. Sometimes called the barrel cactus, they are usually globular or spherical with well-defined ridges and stout, curved or flattened spines which may be tinted. Bloom seasonally with yellow flowers.

Lobivia. Generally round in shape, medium in size and extremely spiny. Produce offsets at the base and, depending upon the species, large flowers which run the gamut from pink to red and from yellow to orange.

Mammillaria. Often called pincushion cacti because of their small cylindrical or globular shape and profusion of spines which give the appearance of a pin-studded pincushion. Characteristic of most species is the development of spiral rows of tubercles as opposed to straight ribs, with an areole in the center of each tubercle. Flowers are generally small but abundant and are arranged in rings around the plant near the top. Colors range from pink to red and white to yellow, depending upon the specie.

Notocactus. Most species are globular, but a few are columnar. This genus is prized for its colorful wiry spines, and the beautiful flowers the various species produce in a wide array of color are considered a bonus. Need richer soil than most cacti.

Opuntia. A large family of cacti that thrive throughout North and South America. Some species have broad flat joints (prickly pear) and others cylindrical or globular joints (cholla). An easily recognized feature of the genus is that each areole puts out tufts of bristles (glochids) which seem to penetrate the human hand with almost perverse eagerness if the plant is not handled with a newspaper or other safety device. Flowers of the many species are yellow and red. Two frequently collected species are *O. ficusindica*, or Indian fig, which in its native habitat is grown for its edible, tasty fruit; and *O. microdasya*, or bunny's ears, which is smaller, more manageable, has no spines and produces yellow blossoms.

Trichnocereus. This genus is indigenous to South America. The various species are columnar in form and branch from the base. Older specimens produce large aromatic white flowers at night, in season.

Basic care for desert cacti. *Soil.* A mix of one part coarse sharp builder's sand or gravel, one part sandy soil, and one part limestone is fairly close to the native soil most desert cacti thrive in. It is not beneficial to add organic matter to the mix and may only serve to hold excessive moisture in the soil which can rot the plant. *Light.* Almost without exception, desert cacti must have a minimum of six hours direct sun to fully develop and bloom. Provide some cross ventilation during the day if the plant is sitting in blazing sunlight. *Water* only when the soil is dry and hard, and then only on a sunny day. The combination of sun and heat pulls out excess moisture from the plant's tissues. A night-watered cactus can't expel this excess and may rot. *Temperature.* Desert cacti like cooler nighttime temperatures but can take high ranges during the day. *Fertilizer.* Feed with a complete water-soluble fertilizer once a year in the peak of the growing season. *Repotting* is usually required only every second or third year. Most cacti do well in smaller pots. *Propagation.* The best propagation method is layering, with stem cuttings a close second. (See techniques under basic care for succulents.)

Jungle cacti. *Epiphyllum*, or orchid cacti. Almost all species are epiphytic (growing on a "host" plant but not absorbing nourishment from it). Stems, which may extend outward and downward a foot or more, are smooth, flat and usually notched or serrated on the edges. The brief blooming season (April through June) produces medium-to-large flowers in almost every hue except blue.

Rhipsalidopsis, a Brazilian native, bears some similarity to the *Schlumbergera bridgesii*, or Christmas cactus. It is angular with short dark green or reddish stems, and is also epiphytic. Blooms in early spring and, occasionally, in September, with red or pink flowers two to three inches long.

Schlumbergera have flat strap-like jointed stems and *S. bridgesii*, or Christmas cactus, throws beautiful carmine-red tubular flowers at Christmas time.

Basic care for jungle cacti. *Soil.* Jungle cacti do best in a composition of one part sharp builder's sand, one part sandy soil, one part peat moss or leaf mold, and some charcoal and redwood bark. *Light.* Most species want a bright window which admits sun filtered through a thin curtain. Direct sun will often burn the leaves. Most can, however, take full winter sun. *Water.* Keep the soil barely moist during the growing season, then slightly drier, but never let the soil completely dry out. *Temperature.* Normal household ranges are adequate. *Fertilizer.* Spring through fall, feed bi-monthly with a complete fertilizer diluted half strength. Withhold fertilizer through the winter. *Re-potting* is seldom called for oftener than every second or third year, if that often. *Propagation.* By seed, stem cuttings or layering. (See techniques under basic care for succulents.)

Chapter 9

Herbs—A Cook's Tour

Herb growing for culinary uses is enjoying a resurgence of popularity in the United States unequalled since Colonial days, when herbs were widely used as seasoning and for preservatives in almost every New England kitchen. The use of herbs reaches back to antiquity—at least as far back as the dawn of civilization. There are poetic references to herbs in both ancient Greek and Roman literature and in the Bible.

Over the centuries, herbs were used in religious ceremonies, in medications, as amulets, in black magic, and in witchcraft rituals. Even to this day, in unenlightened parts of the world, there is a great deal of mysticism attached to herbs and their power to call up and manipulate the Forces of Darkness to do one's evil bidding. But, for our exploration, we shall stick to the more practical and, perhaps, mundane path that leads to achieving a passing familiarity with the culinary applications of herbs.

WHAT IS AN HERB?

Different cultures and countries disagree, as you might expect. What is an herb to a French gourmet cook may be a noxious weed to a Chinese housewife. The word herb comes from the Latin *herba*, which means grass. The classical botanical definition is: "A non-woody perennial, annual or biennial plant that dies to the ground after blossoming each year." This definition is a bit imprecise for it excludes two woody herbs—laurel and rosemary.

A loose but, perhaps, a more realistic definition is: "Any plant whose leaves and seeds are used for flavoring in cooking, for fragrance, or for medicinal purposes." But, even this definition is not totally satisfactory. It excludes roses (the source of rose hips) and

some herbs—anise, for one—whose roots are edible.

So, finally, it becomes apparent that there is no really conclusive definition. Our most reliable guideline to defining which plants are herbs, which are spices and which are other species are the various herbals, or books on herbs, which describe plants used as herbs from earliest recorded history to the present day.

HERB GROWING

Since most herbs grew wild (and many still do) before they were domesticated, with some considered as useless weeds by farmers, they are extremely hardy and often thrive in soil that seems hardly capable of sustaining any plant life. Because of their easy adaptability, almost every herb grows equally well indoors or out. The only requisite for most to flourish indoors is a minimum of six hours of direct sun each day. This presents no problem for most herb-growers in the summer when days are long and there are up to 12 hours of sun. With the advent of winter, though, most herb-fanciers limit their cultivation of herbs to those which can survive with very little sun, or without sun, altogether. Some of these shade-tolerant herbs are angelica, borage, chervil and the various mints.

The section on growing individual herbs gives detailed information on the culture requirements of each of several popular species.

INDOOR HERB GARDENS

Herbs, like most plants, grow well in just about any container—clay, ceramic, plastic, wood, etc. Many cooks prefer a dry-welled pot (without a drainage hole) to hold various herbs, since there is no danger of water damage and they can set the container wherever

59

it's conveniently at hand. This can create a problem. Virtually all herbs need a fast-draining soil which doesn't trap and hold excess water. Since it is difficult to gauge the water volume required to nourish a plant potted in a dry-welled container and, at the same time, not build up a reservoir of water in the bottom of the pot, the risk of creating a bog which will rot the roots is great.

Of course, one can experiment by gradually increasing the amount of water given until the right volume is achieved, but this seems needlessly bothersome. Besides, there is a peculiarly unpleasant, swamp-like odor about a dry-welled plant which comes from soil that is kept continually damp. Even terrariums that are aired periodically are plagued by this pungent, stagnant smell.

As with the cultivation of most indoor plants, terra cotta pots seem to produce the best results. An efficient, attractive and easy-to-care-for herb garden can be created very simply. Pot up a selection of herbs in individual 3″ or 4″ clay pots. Either filch from the kitchen or buy a Teflon-coated cookie sheet (actually, a tray) which has raised sides all around and pour in a layer of aquarium tank pebbles, gravel, or even coarse sand. Set the pots on the gravel and place the tray in a sunny location. The tray will catch excess water which drains through the pots and the Teflon coating will prevent the water from rusting the tray. Let the excess water remain in the pebbles. This creates a beneficial microclimate which helps raise the humidity around the herbs, which is especially good on hot, sunny summer days.

Another popular method is to pot up together several herbs which require similar care and conditions in a terra cotta strawberry pot or a hanging clay or wooden basket. Ideal plants for hanging herb gardens are the trailing varieties such as dittany, rosemary and thyme.

HERB SEEDS—WHEN TO HARVEST

Many of the culinary herbs produce seeds which are used in cooking and for propaga-tion. Anise, caraway and coriander are three of these. Seeds which will be used in cooking should be left on the plant until the pod or head has begun to brown off. Wait for a warm day, then cut the seed head off into a paper bag.

Seeds for propagation should be removed when the heads have turned yellow.

DRYING HERB LEAVES AND SEEDS

Most herbs are useful dried, as well as fresh, and seeds for culinary use are always dried for storage. First, gently wash the herbs by letting warm tapwater run over them for a few minutes, then blot the plants with paper towels to remove excess water. Since dried herbs must be stored in airtight containers to preserve their fresh flavor, all moisture must be removed or they will decay or mold will form on them.

Sunlight burns drying leaves and robs them of their seasoning properties, so drying must be done in the shade where the air temperature is warm and dry. An effective drying technique is to gather branches together in a bunch, tie them at one end, and hang them from the kitchen ceiling or a shaded area of a porch or patio. If the drying is done outdoors, bring in the herbs at night to prevent dew from settling on them. In a few days, the leaves should be crackling dry and can be gently removed from the stems.

Seeds and individual leaves can be dried by placing them on an anti-splatter screen (the type that fits over a skillet) set over a pan, so that air can circulate all around. Leaves should be turned over daily so that the drying process is even.

STORING DRIED HERBS

Almost any container can be used to store herb leaves and seeds, so long as it is airtight. Leaves should be stored whole since they seem to hold their flavor longer if they are not shredded or broken. Label and date the container and store in a cool, dark (if the container is clear glass) place.

The life of dried herbs varies. Chervil, chives, parsley and savory retain their flavor for 9 to 13 months; basil, marjoram, mint, rosemary, thyme, may last as long as a year and a half. Play it safe and check the taste and aroma of dried herbs brought from storage before you use them.

FREEZING HERBS

Herbs can be frozen and preserved in their fresh condition indefinitely until you need them in your culinary excursions. Wash chives, basil and dill in warm water, blot between two layers of paper towel, fold into foil packets, label, date and freeze.

Other herbs should be scalded before freezing. Take a sprig of herbs by the end of the stem with a pair of tongs and dash them several times in boiling water, followed by a cool water rinse. Blot dry with a paper towel, wrap in foil, label, date and freeze.

Popular Culinary Herbs

Anise (Pimpinella anisum) *Annual.* The distinctive licorice flavor of both leaves and seeds of the anise plant adds a piquancy to many foods. Fresh anise leaves in salads lend an unusual taste which can be a welcome change. Anise seeds may be used in cookies and pastries and blended in various cheeses.

How to grow: Use a basic soil mix and keep it barely moist. Full sun for a minimum of six hours a day. Harvest seeds for cooking when the heads brown off—for propagation when heads begin to yellow. Cut leaves as you prepare salad.

Basil (Ocimum basilicum) *Annual.* Of the many species, *O. basilicum* is the most popular for culinary uses. Its sharp, clove-like flavor improves the taste of fish, curries, sauces, dips, poultry, salads and tomato pastes. Its flavor intensifies when cooked, so use it sparingly.

How to grow: Add an extra handful of either peat moss or leaf mold to a basic soil mix and keep it evenly moist. Full sun for a minimum of six hours daily. Sweet basil produces small white flowers which should be pinched out as buds to encourage fullness in the foliage. Propagate from seeds.

Lemon balm (Melissa officinalis) *Perennial. M. officinalis* is favored for its delicate lemon aroma and flavor which enhances soups, stews, fruit salads and as a garnish in claret cups and punchbowls. A pleasant lemony tea can be brewed using young leaves stewed in boiling water.

How to grow: A basic soil mix laced with extra peat moss or leaf mold is ideal. Keep the soil barely moist. Does well with only two to three hours of sun, but the minimum requirement is bright, diffused light. Cut back periodically to maintain control. Propagate from cuttings and by root division.

Borage (Borago officinalis) *Annual.* The cucumber-flavored leaves and the pink and blue, star-shaped flowers of the borage plant impart a hearty flavor to salads. The leaves are also often stewed and served (like collard greens) as a vegetable.

How to grow: Thrives in a basic soil mix. Allow topsoil to dry slightly between waterings. Needs only an hour or two of full sun daily, but bright, diffuse light all day. Propagate from seeds.

Caraway (Carum carvi) *Biennial.* You can use all of the caraway plant for culinary purposes. The root provides a sweet vegetable, the leaves add a delicate flavor to salads and vegetables, such as cabbage and potatoes, and its seeds have long been used in breads, pastries and served with baked apples.

How to grow: Caraway requires two years to mature. The second year produces clusters of white flowers tinged with green and soon seeds develop. Harvest these when they've ripened. Take the delicate leaves as you need them. Leaves for salads should be slightly chilled. Caraway does well in a basic soil mix kept just moist. Needs full sun for a minimum of six hours daily. Propagate from seeds.

Chervil (Anthriscus cerefolium) *Annual.* Primarily, chervil is used as a flavor enhancer to bring out the flavors of other herbs. Also it is one of the ingredients in Bernaise sauce and its leaves, which have some of the flavor of anise, are used in fresh salads.

How to grow: Plant chervil in any good basic soil mix and keep it evenly moist. The delicate, parsley-like foliage suffers from too much sun—an hour or two a day may often wilt the foliage—but give it good, bright, diffuse light all day. Snip out the white flower buds (and even stems) before flowers appear to promote bushiness. Propagate from seeds.

Chives (Allium schoenoprasum) *Perennial.* Almost every cook, amateur or professional, is familiar with the versatility of this oniony plant. It perks up salads and dressings, dips, sauces for fish, egg dishes and omelets, grilled cheese sandwiches, etc., etc.

How to grow: Use a basic soil mix laced with extra peat moss or leaf mold and keep it moist. A minimum of six hours sun intensifies the flavor, but it will survive in bright, diffuse light. The purple flowers it produces should be "nipped in the bud" because they rob the leaves of tenderness. Propagate from seeds or by root division. Indoors, the plant is evergreen so there is always an abundant supply.

Dill (Anethum graveolens) *Annual.* Dill has more going for it than just pickling. Try its leaves and seeds with boiled potatoes, with lamb, fish, poultry, in sauces for meats and salads and its seeds in breads, since the latter are similar in flavor to caraway.

How to grow: Basic soil mix. Allow topsoil to dry out between waterings. Requires at least six hours of sun daily. Harvest seeds in fall or plant will self-sow. Propagate from seeds.

Marjoram (Majorana hortensis) *Perennial.* Marjoram is used to season soups, sauces, stews, pastes, in jellies, dumplings, biscuits, meat dishes, casseroles and in vinegar.

How to grow: Add a pinch or two of peat moss to a basic soil mix and keep it evenly moist. Full sun is required for it to thrive. Trim the plant occasionally and remove buds for control and to improve the texture of leaves. Propagate from seeds in spring, or from stem cuttings or root division.

Oregano (Origanum vulgare) *Perennial.* Commonly called wild marjoram, oregano was virtually unknown in this country, except by gourmet cooks, until the 1940's. It was in Italy that American soldiers were introduced to the herb, which is similar in taste to thyme, in Italian dishes. It is a prime ingredient, also, in Spanish and Mexican fare—sauces, beans, meats, eggs and cheese.

How to grow: Does well in a basic soil mix kept on the dry side. Give it full sun for at least six hours a day. Pinch out flower buds to encourage fullness and tender foliage. Propagate from seeds or cuttings.

Rosemary (Rosmarinum officinalis) *Perennial.* Rosemary leaves, either dried or fresh, perk up stews, vegetables, poultry (in stuffing), and meats. They also help create a zesty basting sauce for such things as roast lamb and pork.

How to grow: Rosemary will grow in almost any soil, so a basic soil mix is suitable. Keep it on the dry side—to a depth of about an inch below the surface. Give it all the sun you can. It becomes stunted in poor light. Propagate from seeds or stem cuttings.

Sage (Salvia) *Perennial.* Sage leaves, both fresh and dried, treat the palate in meat stuffings, sausage, in the basting sauce for baked fish, in dips and with roast goose.

How to grow: Thrives in a basic soil mix

kept on the dry side. Allow the topsoil to dry out between waterings. Sun, for a minimum of six hours daily, is required for this herb to grow well. Propagate from seeds or cuttings.

Thyme (Thymus vulgaris) *Perennial.* Thyme's strong, pervasive flavor, if the herb is used sparingly, adds a zippy taste to fish, poultry and poultry stuffings, to cottage cheese, salads and vegetable juices, to name only a few. Use the leaves fresh or dried.

How to grow: Use a basic soil mix and water only when the soil is dry a quarter to a half an inch below the surface. To maintain control and promote bushiness, selectively snip out some growing tips. Propagate from seeds and cuttings.

Other Herbs for Culinary Uses

Angelica (Angelica archangelica) *Biennial.* All parts are useful. The stems and roots may be boiled and eaten as an unusual vegetable, and the seeds can be brewed to make angelica tea.

Burnet (Sanguisorba minor) *Perennial.* Fresh, young burnet leaves have a nutty, cucumber-like flavor which makes them a natural for fresh salads.

Catnip (Nepeta cataria) *Perennial.* In addition to sending cats on a "trip," catnip makes a pleasant-tasting tea rich in vitamins A and C.

Coriander (Coriandrum sativum) *Annual.* The pungent leaves of coriander (sometimes called Chinese parsley or cilantro) are frequently used by gourmet cooks in the preparation of fowl, sausage and spicy meat dishes. Chinese cooks use coriander in zesty soups. Ground coriander seeds are used in pastries and puddings.

Fennel (Foeniculum vulgare) *Perennial.* Used as a seasoning for roast pork, fish dishes, cheeses, vegetables and pastries. It imparts a slightly licorice flavor, akin to anise.

Tarragon (Artemisia dracunculus) *Perennial.* Used fresh or dried in roast chicken, egg dishes, fish and salads. Also used in vinegar preparations.

Chapter 10

Terrariums And Bottle Gardens

With the exception of a cactus collection, terrariums and bottle gardens are the easiest indoor "gardens" to care for. Since the plants are encased in glass they are not affected, as are other houseplants, by the hot dry air and temperature fluctuations which prevail in most homes. The air inside the glass container is continually warm and moist, similar to that of a greenhouse, creating an ideal microclimate for many tropical and subtropical plants

Only two things are required for terrarium and bottle garden plants to thrive: (1) Good light (no direct sun), which means a position near a window with northern exposure or drapes which admit strong but diffuse light. (2) Enough moisture to keep the air inside humid.

After the initial watering, when the terrarium is planted, all that is needed is an occasional water misting with a hand atomizer. For weeks afterward, water vapor that is thrown off by the plants (technical term, *transpiration*) collects on the inside and trickles back down on the plants, automatically providing nourishment and moisture. Only when you notice that moisture is no longer condensing on the interior walls do you mist again, and this is usually weeks later.

Parents who want to teach their children about nature and imbue them with an appreciation of growing things frequently find the creation of bottle gardens and terrariums an ideal educative tool. Children, as any parent knows, are inherently very impatient. If they plant some seeds this morning they expect to see Jack-in-the-Beanstalk results by lunchtime. When nothing visible happens for days or weeks, they often lose interest in all future botanical projects, regardless of parental cajoling and promises of bountiful vegetation.

But, the bottle garden or terrarium produces immediate results. The plants begin to thrive from the moment they are transplanted. Each day those curious little eyes can check on the progress of their garden and enjoy the beauty and sense of accomplishment it affords.

Terrariums are simpler to construct than bottle gardens because you have a larger opening and can work inside with your hands. You can also create more realistic woodland scenes in miniature in a terrarium since you can easily add large rocks and branches as landscape accents.

Materials. *Container.* Virtually any watertight glass or plastic container will serve, as long as the material is not too deeply tinted. Lightly-tinted glass or slightly "smoked" plastic, however, still admit sufficient light for plants to flourish. You can use aquarium tanks, glass bowls, brandy snifters, bottles or containers made of acrylic. You can even make your own container from sheet acrylic cut, shaped (by heat), and glued into almost any configuration you want. Large hobby shops are good sources for sheet acrylic and information on construction techniques.

Lid. Anything that fits snugly over the opening of the container is fine, even polyethylene fastened with a rubberband. For aquarium tanks, 10-gallon size and under, you can get a sheet of glass cut exactly to size for about a dollar at almost any hardware or lumber/building supply store. Ask the proprietor to dull the edges, since you'll be handling the lid often and can easily slice a finger. If he is reluctant to do it for you, do it yourself with sandpaper or a file. Obviously, you'll want to wear gloves for this operation.

Step 1. Thoroughly clean and polish terrarium container.

Step 2. Lay out the materials and tools you'll need.

Step 3. Pour in a layer of charcoal to keep the soil sweet and to neutralize decomposition gases.

Step 4. Next, add gravel to a depth of one to two inches.

Step 5. Add soil mixture.

Step 6. Pack down soil. Create hills and valleys for realistic landscape effect.

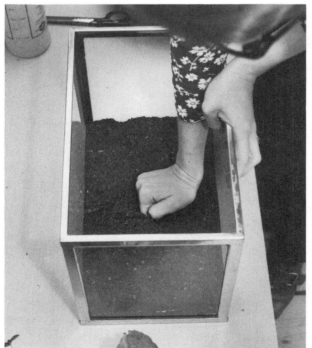

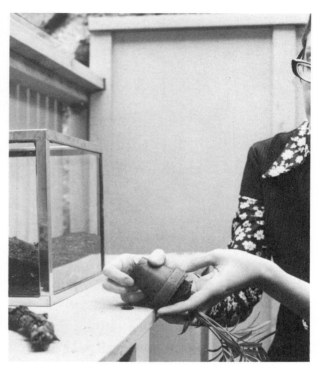

Step 7. Knock out first plant.

Step 8. Position plant and follow same procedure until all plants are positioned.

Add rocks and branches for woodland accents.

Step 10. Mist foliage thoroughly.

Step 9. Remove dead or yellow foliage.

Step 11. Add water to moisten dry areas, then cover with lid.

The safest technique is to place newspaper on a table, then lay the glass flat on it, with one edge extending slightly over the end of the table. Hold the glass down firmly with one hand and sand or file each edge individually.

Soil and amendments. You'll need horticultural *charcoal* to neutralize fumes created by decay and, thus, to keep the soil "sweet;" *sand* or *gravel* to form a dry well into which excess water can drain; enough *soil* to provide adequate growing room for plant roots; and, finally, sphagnum *moss*, to line the container's inside if you wish to hide the potting media.

The soil "recipe" is important. It shouldn't be overly rich in nutrients since this would induce the plants to "take off" and soon outgrow their container. A good custom-mix soil recipe is one part pasteurized sandy soil or loam, two parts coarse sand, and one part leaf mold. Soil for all plants, and terrariums in particular, should be pasteurized to kill any fungi, larvae, grass and weed seeds which would soon take over a terrarium because of the ideal climate. Most commercially-packaged soils are pasteurized, but it's always wise to check the label to make sure.

Miscellaneous. Choose rocks and branches for their shape and character. The rocks should resemble boulders and the branches should call to mind fallen logs such as you might find in a forest.

Plants. Terrarium and bottle garden plants should be slow-growers in dish-garden size, so they won't outstrip the confines of the container for at least a year, preferably longer. The following are all ideal specimens for terrariums and bottle gardens: Maidenhair fern (*Adiantum pedatum*), table ferns (*Pteris*), trailing arbutus (*Epigaea repens*), partridge-berry (*Mitchella repens*), parlor palm (*Neanthe bella*), peperomia, fittonia, begonia, goldthread (*Coptis trifolia*), wintergreen (*Pyrola elliptica*), common and striped pipsissewas (*Chimaphila*), rattlesnake plantain (*Goodyera pubescens*), and *Polypodium vulgare*.

To create a really striking, professional-looking terrarium select only four or five species in different heights, rather than all of one kind or a dozen different specimens.

Preparation. The container should be clean when you begin. Glass should be washed inside and out with hot soapy water, rinsed and wiped dry with a lint-free cloth. Clean acrylic with either soap and water or a spray-type window cleaner. Lay out all the materials you'll be using so that everything is close at hand. Next, visualize how you want the finished terrarium to look. It may even be a good idea to sketch a landscaping plan to follow. Finally, water the plants a few hours before you intend to transfer them to the terrarium so they will knock out of their pots easily.

How to plant. (1) Spread sphagnum moss over the bottom and up the sides of the container, if you want to hide the charcoal, gravel and soil. (2) Pour in a layer of charcoal to a depth of half to three quarters of an inch. (3) Add a layer of gravel or sand one to two inches deep. (4) Add the soil mixture and pack it down with your knuckles. During steps (3) and (4), you should be shaping and forming hills and valleys as you add these materials, if you want to create a more interesting woodland scene. (5) Knock out the first plant and position it in the space you've chosen, then follow the same procedure until all the plants are in place.

If you feel you may want to rearrange or change plants from time to time, leave them in their pots and set the plant, pot and all, in the container. The pot can be hidden by covering it with sphagnum moss. Otherwise, knock the plants out one by one as you transfer them to the terrarium. (6) Next, trim off any dead, damaged or yellowing foliage and wipe down the inside of the container with a lint-free cloth. (7) Mist all the foliage lightly and spoon in just enough water to moisten any overly-dry areas. Too much water can rot the plants, sour the soil and encourage the formation of mold. (8) Finally, cover with the

lid and set the terrarium in a shaded place for a few days to help the newly-transplanted plants get established, then move to a well-illuminated (no sun!) location. If the inside fogs up from moisture condensation the first few days, slide the lid back about an inch for a few hours each day. This will allow the excess moisture to evaporate and the soil to dry out slightly. After a week or ten days, the moisture content inside should reach an ideal level (provided you haven't been overly generous with the water) and you can leave the lid in place for long periods.

Bottle Gardens require more time and patience to construct because of the small opening through which foliage, root ball and materials must pass. The materials required are more or less the same as terrariums, except for three additional tools. To keep the interior walls of the bottle relatively clean as you add charcoal, gravel, and soil, you'll need a *funnel* when you pour. A long section of dowel, which is available at lumber yards and hardware stores, or even a stick, can be used as a *tamping tool* to firm the soil and create hills and valleys. You'll also need a spring-action *pick-up tool*, which is available at hardware stores for about $3, to insert and position plants.

How to plant. Follow steps (1) through (4) described under terrarium-building, except use your tamping tool to form and pack the soil. Next, knock out the first plant and remove most of the soil from the root ball. Curl

70

the roots inward so that they will pass safely through the opening and grasp the stem with the pick-up tool. Insert the plant into the bottle and lay it on its side where you intend to position it. Using your tamping tool, spread the roots and use your pick-up tool to right the plant while you tamp soil around the roots.

When the bottle garden is complete, pour a small amount of water into the opening, allowing it to trickle down the inside neck and walls to flush down soil and other debris. Don't overdo the irrigation, since moisture in a bottle garden takes two to three times as long to evaporate as it does in a conventional terrarium.

Chapter 11

Dollar-Stretchers, Miscellany And Serendipity

Second Hand, Rose? If you have more time than money, or you prefer to spend your horticultural budget mostly on plants, you may want to consider picking up your pots (and even gardening implements) at one of the many thrift and charity retail outlets. Goodwill Industries and The Salvation Army both operate thrift shops in almost every community across the country. You can usually find a good selection of plastic and terra cotta containers which sold new for 50¢ up to $8 for 10¢ to 25¢ apiece. Avoid those with cracks (roots can grow into them and get pinched, and they tend to leak water) and those so heavily encrusted with salts and algae that you can't see the clay beneath.

Obviously, you'll have to scrub the terra cotta pots clean before you use them, and it's quite a job. The best way to tackle it is to fill a bucket with a strong solution of TSP diluted in hot water. Place the pots in the bucket and let them soak for an hour or two to soften some of the patina. Put on a pair of sturdy rubber gloves (TSP is mildly irritating to tender skin) and, one by one, scrub the pots with coarse (No. 3) steel wool or a stiff wire brush. Since they get a bit slippery and hard to handle, the most productive technique is to turn the pots upsidedown on newspapers and work down from the base. A little scouring powder is helpful, also. Rinse the finished pots in clean water to remove all traces of the chemicals and allow them to air dry thoroughly before you plant in them.

Roll in the barrel. City apartments really put an indoor gardener's ingenuity to supreme tests. Without a patio or balcony, there just isn't any really satisfactory place to pot up, mix soil, or perform any of the dozens of horticultural chores which are required from time to time. Then, there is the problem of materials storage. Where does one stash all the gear, soil, pots, etc., which increase in bulk and variety over the years? Most apartments are woefully lacking in adequate storage space (or closets!).

When I lived in an urban high rise, I solved this problem by purchasing a medium-sized fibre barrel with a tight-fitting lid from a local barrel manufacturer. I painted the outside a semi-gloss white (oil base paint that is scrubbable) to match the kitchen wall (the inside is usually coated with a plastic varnish) and stored all my horticultural paraphernalia inside. Seldom-used chemicals, extra pots (stacked one inside the other) and the like went in the bottom. Soil, peat moss, etc., I kept in individual plastic bags tightly sealed with twist-ties to retain their moisture content. Tamping tools, trowels, etc., went inside my soil-mixing bucket to keep them from straying and to conserve space. With the lid on, I had a small but adequate work space, and when I was finished, the barrel became a plant stand for my large *Cissus rhombifolia* (grape ivy) which trailed magnificently down the sides.

Barrels in paper, fibre, or metal come in almost any size, from one-foot diameter by two feet high, up to the industrial-size giants which are really 50-gallon drums. Manufacturers and outlets are listed under "Barrels" in the yellow pages of your phone directory.

Ring around the carpet. A common problem most indoor gardeners face is damage from moisture residue which has leeched through terra cotta saucers under plants. Continually damp clay saucers can mildew carpets and stain or warp vinyl tile or wood floors. Only ceramic tile floors are impervious to permanent damage. In the last few years, a few pottery manufacturers have in-

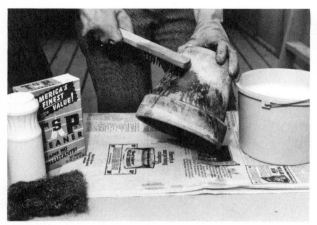

Scrub with a wire brush or steel wool.

Pot is now clean and ready to plant in.

troduced terra cotta saucers which are glazed on the inside so that moisture can't leech through. These solve the water-damage problem, but these glazed saucers cost two to three times more than unglazed.

One solution I've found to achieve a watertight effect in saucers for only a few cents per saucer is to coat the inside with a masonry sealer. Try a hardware or building supply firm. I've never been able to achieve a permanent bond between terra cotta and paint, lacquer, varnish, or anything other than the masonry sealer.

Another "homemade" product I find useful both for making heavy plants slide easily when I want to clean under or relocate them, and for protecting floors and furniture from scuffs and scratches, is indoor-outdoor carpet. I buy one-foot squares (available in paint, hardware and carpet stores) for 39¢ and cut them to size by drawing the outline of the saucer with a felt-tip pen, scoring with a single-edged razor blade and finishing the job neatly with an old pair of scissors. The rubberized side goes up against the saucer and the carpet side down on the floor, under the plant. I've also found that the rubber backing is 99% effective in preventing moisture from penetrating.

Mainly for Southern and California folk. Indoor gardeners who live in California or the southern U.S. have an advantage over those who are located in the north, in one regard. Many of the specimens which are universally sold in the warm-belt region as houseplants are also sold as outdoor landscaping plants. This includes such tropicals as *Ficus elastica* (rubber tree), *Ficus benjamina* (weeping fig), and *Philodendron selloum*. Nurseries sell these plants inside as houseplants and outside as outdoor plants. Invariably, the plants found inside are often $10 to $15 more than their counterparts outside. The difference, of course, is that the plants sold inside are hothouse grown and adapt easily to an interior environment. The plants outside were "field grown" and are acclimated to temperature extremes, sun, etc. Admittedly, it is far simpler to pay the difference in price and get a plant that is free of problems, but most of us who buy a new specimen every week or two would soon run short of funds. Plant-collecting is habit-forming and all of us run the risk of becoming, if you'll pardon a terrible pun, plantaholics.

So, for those who live in the warm-belt, the most economical way to build an enviable plant collection is to purchase outdoor plants and adapt them to an indoor environment.

Acclimating plants to a new environment is easier than it may seem—but only if you're patient. You can't rush it.

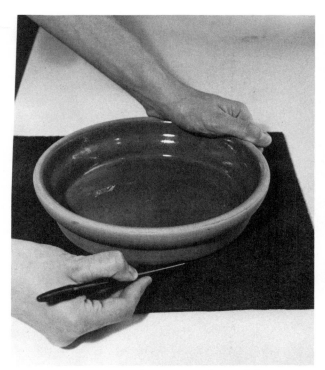

Using a felt-tip pen, draw an outline of the saucer base on either side of the carpet tile.

Cut the pattern out with an old pair of scissors.

Slip under pot, rubber side up, carpet side down.

First, let's take *outdoor-to-indoor*. If the plant was in full sun at the nursery, move it into partial shade for a few days (seven to ten days should be sufficient). If it adjusts to this location without difficulty, move it into full shade for another week. Again, if it adapts well, move it inside. First, select a temporary spot near a north or east window. Leave it there for ten days to two weeks, keeping the air cool (under 70°) and the humidity high during this period. If no drooping of leaves or branches occurs, no leaves fall, and the plant continues to look strong and healthy after the interior adjustment period, you've got yourself a bargain houseplant. You may leave it where it is or move it to any other area which gets good light all day and you need no longer worry about temperature. It can now adjust to the normal temperature fluctuations of your interior environment.

If you should lose some leaves during the acclimation process it isn't a panic situation, unless it's obvious from the appearance of the

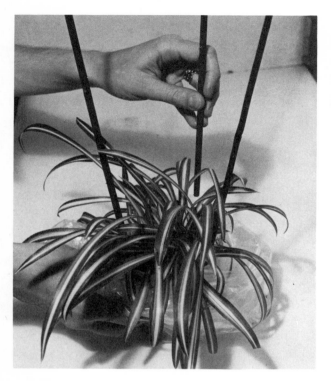

Preparing a plant to survive while you're on vacation is fairly simple. Insert three bamboo stakes around the inside rim of the pot, water and mist.

Put the plant in the bottom of a plastic bag.

Pull bag up over the pot and stakes and tie securely. Set the plant in a shady spot inside (never in the sun!). The plant should survive in its miniature greenhouse for up to three weeks, often longer.

rest of the foliage that the entire plant is deteriorating. Sometimes a plant will drop a few leaves from temporary shock, but new leaves immediately form and grow to maturity. Very seldom does a plant collapse from an environmental change of outside to inside (unless the air is continuously hot and dry) but it often occurs in the reverse, if care is not taken.

A few words of caution: Be especially watchful for evidence of pest infestation with field-grown plants. Since they've been exposed to a myriad of predators, you may find some strange critters doing numbers to the foliage. Identify the invaders either by matching them up with your trusty plant pest reference, so you'll know how to cope, or take one to your nurseryman and ask him for advice. Some horticulturalists advise pouring insecticide into the soil of any plant you buy, "just in case." I feel this is a bad habit to get into. Insecticides should not be used frivolously. Besides, the plant may not be contaminated at all, or the worst it has may be only an errant slug which can be easily removed.

Inside-to-outside is trickier, particularly if the plant has never had to survive outside. A plant that has adjusted to the minimal temperature variations and low light level of the average interior does not take kindly to being relegated to the harsh outdoors. The most advantageous time to attempt this is in the late spring, when all danger of frost is passed, when the night temperature remains relatively pleasant, and when the plant is entering its active growth period.

The process must be a gradual one. First, situate the plant in a shaded area and only keep it outside during the warmest hours of the day. Gradually extend the length of time each day until, finally, it can survive permanently outdoors. Even then, make sure it is not in direct sunlight, or it will collapse. Dappled shade is fine, provided the plant agrees. Almost never, though, will a houseplant adapt to a full-sun situation. Since most are tropicals, they come from humid, shaded jungle floors where the sun seldom penetrates.

For the complete story on adapting outdoor plants to grow into beautiful shrubs and trees in your living room, read my new book, "*Big Plants for Small Budgets—How to Grow Outdoor Plants Indoors*" (Chronicle Books, San Francisco, $4.95). I describe fifty traditional outdoor plants, most of which need little acclimation to thrive in your home.

Something for those in cooler climes. Houseplant aficionados whose geographical locations rule out easy access to inexpensive field-grown tropicals shouldn't despair. If you are a Minnesotan or upstate New Yorker, you are not totally devoid of opportunities to acquire and adapt traditional outdoor plants, shrubs, and even trees to interior environments. There are several specimens which have been grown successfully indoors (often by novices who didn't know they couldn't do it). Some of these are bamboo, bougainvillea, coffee tree (*Coffea arabica*), fig tree (*Ficus carica*), Japanese maple (*Acer palmatum*), dwarf mandarin orange, Meyer lemon, lime tree, tangelo tree, and Pigmy date palm (*Phoenix roebelenii*). Both bougainvillea and maple are deciduous and drop their leaves seasonally, but there have been cases where maples have kept their leaves nearly through a long winter. (I'm firmly convinced that, under the right conditions, *anything* that grows outdoors will survive indoors.)

If you like flowering plants, there are several species, with more being developed and marketed every year, which will bloom readily in a sunny winter window. If geraniums are to your taste, you can adapt them to thrive and bloom all winter indoors simply by pinching out the buds before they open during the summer, then bringing them inside and letting them go to bloom in a sun-drenched area.

Beautiful plants from humble beginnings. There are ways to own handsome, expensive-looking and, sometimes, exotic indoor plants for a minimal financial outlay—but a considerable investment of time.

Ideas for everyone. An unexploited source for veritable jungles of lush, green foliage (and, maybe even flowers) to brighten a dull winter window is at your disposal—*in* your disposal. Retrive the pits and seeds of such things as avocado, olive, papaya, mango, and pot them up. Most are fast growers and, will give you dramatic and impressive plants and trees.

There is a delightful informative book which gives step-by-step instructions for transforming homely seeds and pits from fruits (even bananas) into beautiful houseplants, written by a New Yorker who has done horticultural wonders in his city apartment. It's called *The After-Dinner Gardening Book*, by Richard W. Langer (Macmillan, $4.95).

Chapter 12

Some Choice Houseplants
And
How To Grow Them

Araucaria excelsa

(ar-uh-KAY'ree-uh ex-SELL'suh)
Common Names: Norfolk Island pine;
Star pine
Nativity: Norfolk Island, South Pacific

This beautiful evergreen member of the pine family is seldom grown indoors because of the natural assumption that pines do not thrive indoors. This one does. It's a slow-grower but eventually develops into a dramatic, stylized, living Christmas tree with branches densely covered with half-inch-long needles. As a seedling, it grows in almost symmetrical perfection, with overlapping branches. In its native habitat, trees several decades old reach 200 feet; indoors, five or six feet can be expected after several years. Pruning or heading back will ruin this plant. Once the growing tips are cut, they're never replaced, permanently distorting the shape of the tree. **Price:** Generally available in one-gallon cans for $2.50 to $4.95 and five-gallon cans at $7.95 to $9.50 at many nurseries. Potted specimens, three to four feet, range from $15 to $35.

Basic care: Does best in a slightly acid soil mix. Water when the soil is dry one inch below the surface, and never let the soil completely dry out. Thrives in a cool environment, which makes it suitable for air-conditioned interiors, but survives in normal household temperature levels. Tolerates only winter sun, but likes fairly bright natural or artificial light. Try a north exposure window. Feed monthly with a complete fertilizer. Check periodically for pests, particularly for mealybugs which have an affinity for this species.

Asparagus ferns

(as-PAIR'uh-gus)
Common Names: (See below)
Nativity: Primarily South Africa

Of the hundred-plus varieties of asparagus ferns, four adapt well indoors: *A. meyerii*, the plume or foxtail asparagus; *A. plumosus*, the

Araucaria excelsa (Star Pine)

emerald feather; *A. retrofractus*; and, the star of the species, *A. sprengerii*, also known under the stage names Sprenger fern and asparagus plant. All four have foliage characteristics of the species—tiny, needle-thin leaves which are really flat branches technically called *cladodes*. All four are ideal houseplants, especially for those who like to water their plants every few minutes. All can take much more water than most other species, as long as the excess can pass swiftly through the soil and out the drainage hole.

A. meyerii grows in upright, fluffy plumes that may reach three or four feet.

A. plumosus is most commonly available only as a dwarf not exceeding three feet, but the standard variety grows to eighteen feet and averages fifteen. Florists use branches of the dwarf cultivar to enhance floral arrangements.

81

A. retrofractus has the structure of a small tree with a well-developed branching system. Its delicate-looking foliage is carried at the tips of the stems in clusters of tiny leaves. Its natural tendency is toward upright, tree-like growth, but pinching back the growing tips encourages it to fill out and achieve a bushier, shrubby character. New stems are pale green and look very much like thin, elongated asparagus plants. These can be tied down and trained to adapt the plant to a particular space.

A. sprengerii seems to do best as a hanging plant because of its appealing tendency to drop arching stems four to six feet long over the edge of its container, creating a very pleasing cascading effect. Greater fullness can be achieved by pinching back the stems to encourage new stems to develop. The spiny stems of the plant are covered with quarter-inch to half-inch needles. It is an extremely fast grower and produces a striking specimen within only a month or two, with red berries and pink flowers at maturity. If you are after a really full specimen, pot up two or three plants in a large plastic pot (with saucer attached) or wire basket. Remember that hanging plants dry out nearly three times as fast as those situated on the floor because they are completely engulfed by rising warm air. For this reason, most specimens that are suspended from the ceiling or high rafters should be watered every two or three days in hot weather and every five to six days the rest of the year. *A. sprengerii* also does well potted up conventionally in a terra cotta container and kept on a jardiniere. The important thing is to provide some distance between the plant and the floor so it can trail its stems.

Price: If you buy a specimen in a one-gallon or five-gallon can at the nursery, expect to pay $1.98 to $2.50 and $6.95 to $7.50, respectively. Potted specimens with one young plant should be available for about $1 to $3.00; two plants in the pot, $4.95 to $6.

Basic care: A basic soil mix works for all four. Water hanging plants every two or three days in hot weather. "Grounded" specimens should be watered when the topsoil is dry. A north or south window space is the first choice, but all can take some morning sun, winter and summer. The secret is to provide cross ventilation and keep the plants well-watered and misted. Normal household temperatures are satisfactory and all can take cooler conditions—down to 50°. Feed every two weeks from April to August with a complete fertilizer at half strength. Watch for chlorosis (yellowing foliage), especially with *A. sprengerii*. Frequent irrigations wash away nutrients and trace elements. If yellowing occurs, use an iron additive (chelated) to restore green color.

Beaucarnea recurvata (Bottle Palm)

Asparagus meyerii (Plume Asparagus)

Begonia 'Pink Parade'

Beaucarnea recurvata
(bow-CAR'nee-uh re-cur-VOT'uh)
Common Names: Elephant-foot tree;
Bottle palm; Pony tail
Nativity: Mexico and Texas

This botanical oddity is a member of the yucca family and makes a truly unusual indoor plant which is, unfortunately, largely unavailable in most northern and central states. Its characteristics are a swolen wrinkled truck at the soil line which gradually tapers inward, topped by a tuft of grassy leaves half to three-quarters of an inch wide and three to four feet long. It gets its common name from the clumpy, ridged, bulbous trunk which, without too great a stretch of the imagination resembles an elephants's foot. The trunk is composed of water-storing tissues which, camel-like, store water to carry the plant safely through periods of drought in its normally arid natural habitat. This characteristic makes transplanting and repotting a breeze, since the plant can survive for days on its water reservoir if severed from its roots. Older specimens may develop several trunks and can reach 25 feet in height indoors, but 15 feet is average. *B. recurvata* does well in its original pot for several years, but when repotting is necessary, it should be done around March or April, before new growth begins. **Price:** Prices range from $4.95 for a plant in a 4″ pot (about 6″ tall) up to $175 for a mature specimen.

Basic care: *B. recurvata* thrives in a custom soil mix consisting of one part sandy soil (loam), one part leaf mold, one part coarse sand or gravel and two tablespoons of limestone per gallon of mix. Allow the soil to dry out to a depth of two inches below the surface before watering again. Needs bright natural light to really grow well—a sunny summer window shaded by a filmy curtain or a bright window with diffuse light. Can take full direct winter sun. It will survive with less intense illumination, however. Normal interior temperature ranges are ideal, but *B. recurvata* suffers at temperatures above 100°. Feed twice a year, in early spring and late summer, with a complete fertilizer at full strength.

Begonia
(bug-OWN'ih-uh)
Common Names: Many
Nativity: Many warm-climate countries, primarily Africa, Central and South America.

There are well over 6,000 classified species, varieties and hybrids of *Begonias*, with more being added annually by hundreds of plant hybridizers. The generally-accepted horticultural classifications of the three major types are *fibrous-rooted*, which includes wax and angel wing, with little root structure and tall, branching growth; *rhizomatous*, which includes beefsteak and rex, with root-like stems which spread across the surface of the soil and produce no upright branching stems;

84

and the summer-flowering *tuberous-rooted*, which grows from an underground stem called a tuber. Tuberous types seem to be the most reluctant to do well indoors. Two foes of most are dry, arid conditions and direct summer sun. Many *can* take, and even require, some sun to produce their colorful, often delicately-structured flowers which may be white, yellow, pink, or red. One of the appealing features about the plant is that it propagates easily so you may increase your stock rapidly. Many fibrous-rooted, stem-bearing varieties may be propagated from cuttings from half-ripened, woody stems. The rhizomatous varieties are propagated by division of the rhizome and the heavy-leaved types, particularly rex, reproduce from leaf cuttings. Of all the myriad species and cultivars, probably the easiest for novices to cultivate successfully indoors are the ones classified as "semperflorens," which are fibrous-rooted. These seem almost eager to flower abundantly indoors. **Price:** From 49¢ for a tiny specimen and up. Average price for a plant in a six-inch pot is $5.95; a hanging basket usually brings $10 to $15.

Basic care: It is impossible to give precise basic care for the hundreds of *Begonia* cultivars available today. The only reliable guideline you can safely follow is to either research the particular hybrid in a definitive horticultural reference, such as "EXOTICA," or ask the nurseryman or retailer what the plant requires to thrive. The following basic information is applicable to a large percentage of *Begonias* available in this country. If you follow it, you won't go too far afield. Most *Begonias* prefer a basic, well-draining mix that is kept evenly moist in spring and summer (with high humidity) and slightly dry in fall and winter. Most are shallow-rooted, so a container similar to a bulb pan is best. As a general rule, a window that admits curtain-filtered sunlight in summer and full sun in winter is ideal. A temperature range of 65°-75° is recommended. Feed most with a 50% dilution of a complete fertilizer, alter-

Begonia x 'Thurstonii

nating chemical with organic, every three weeks from January to October.

Brassaia actinophylla
(bruh-SAY'ee-uh ac-tin-o-FY'luh)
Also called *Schefflera actinophylla*
Common Names: Umbrella plant;
Australian umbrella tree
Nativity: Australia

One of the most beautiful of all house-plants, the *Schefflera* is still among the top five in demand even after several years of popularity. It does have on unfortunate drawback and that is its susceptibility to spider mite infestation. When discovered, the mite contamination is almost always too severe to combat. Many nurserymen have told me that they find the mite problem insurmountable and have stopped ordering *Scheffleras* from their growers. I lost several,

86

including a seven-foot specimen, before I started applying systemic poison to the soil immediately after acquiring a new specimen. The plant develops horizontal tiers of oval or elliptical leaves creating the effect of an open umbrella. Young specimens throw out six to seven leaves at the end of each branch and, after maturity, sixteen leaves, each of which is roughly two inches wide and 12″ to 14″ long. To frustrate its tendency to go leggy, selectively pinch out new leaf sets before they emerge. You can also cut back the stem successfully. The plant recovers nicely. **Price:** Dish-garden size, 49¢ to 79¢; 6″ pot (about two or three feet tall specimen), $8 to $10; 8″ pot (about four feet), $15 to $25; larger specimens, add $10 a foot.

Basic care: Any good basic soil mix is suitable for *Scheffleras*. Water when topsoil is dry. To discourage spider mites, wash the entire plant weekly with Ivory soap and warm water and mist daily, since mites dislike moisture which wrecks their feeble attempts at web-spinning. Needs strong light, either natural or artificial, but only winter sun. Direct summer sun "bleaches" the leaves and can scorch. Prefers high humidity and warmth. Responds well to grouping with other plants and resting on a saucer of moist pebbles to create a microclimate. Feed monthly from March to August with a complete fertilizer at half strength.

Chamaedorea elegans

(kam-uh-DOR′ee-uh EL′ee-gons)
Also called *Neanthe bella*
Common Name: Parlor palm
Nativity: Mexico to South America

This species has two attractive features to recommend it: (1) It's one of the few easy-maintenance foliage plants, surviving neglect, dust, drought, excess moisture, and cool temperatures (although cold drafts cause the edges of the leaves to brown off). (2) It's relatively inexpensive, even in the larger sizes. It also can remain pot-bound far longer than most plants, and actually benefits from root-crowding. Repotting is necessary only about every three or four years. In appearance, it has the classic palm characteristics—arching fronds of leaves eight to 16 inches long, unfurling from its trunk in typical palm fashion. Normally, a mature specimen grows indoors to 28 inches in height, but a well-grown plant may reach three or even four feet. Outdoors, in temperate areas, growth potential is much greater. *C. elegans* makes a more dramatic accent specimen if three plants are potted up in one container. At maturity, panicles of seeds are produced and these can be sown to increase your stock. Damaged foliage can be cut back anytime of year and will soon be replaced with new growth. **Price:** Dish garden size, for terrariums and bottle gardens, 39¢ to 79¢. Larger sizes, up to three plants in a 6″ pot, $1.79 to $6.95.

Chamaedorea elegans (Parlor Palm)

88

Basic care: Soil recipe should be basic mix or use commercially-prepared mix and add (if needed) leaf mold and some sharp sand. Irrigate when soil is dry half an inch below the surface, but less frequently through the winter. Prefers normal interior temperature ranges, but can take cooler nighttime temperatures (down to 55°). Medium light—10 feet from a north window, for example—is ideal, but will survive with much less or only artificial illumination. Bright light (even winter sun "bleaches" color from the leaves. Feed twice a month from spring to fall with a complete, water-soluble fertilizer at half-strenth. Usually, pests are not a problem with *C. elegans*, but check periodically anyway for scale and mealybugs.

Chlorophytum comosum

(klor-OFF′uh-tum cum-OWE′sum)
Common Names: Spider plant; Ribbon plant
Nativity: South Africa

An easy and worthy relative of the lily family, the "spider plant" sends up an explosion of gracefully-arching green leaves accented with a bold white stripe down the center and, eventually, long runners which trail down and carry either small white flowers or mirror-image reproductions of the mother plant—sometimes both. If left attached, the runners can extend almost ceiling-to-floor, but many gardeners prefer to anchor the "baby spiders" in a small pot (hairpins or bent paper clips are good for this job), and when they're rooted, detach them to increase their stock or to make gift plants. Each infant plant will soon develop into a picture-perfect image of its mother. You may wish to leave the plants attached to the runners. Over the years, they'll increase in size helping create a really striking specimen. It is best to keep the plant in a 5″ pot until it "requests" larger quarters (usually every two or three years) by pushing up out of its pot. This crowding technique encourages a profusion of foliage and hastens maturity. **Price:** In 2″ pots, about $1; in 5″ containers, $3.95 to $5.00. Mature specimens, usually potted up in plastic containers and already rigged for hanging, with several runners two to three feet long, fetch from $10.95 in nurseries to $35 in plant boutiques.

Basic care: Rich fast-draining soil mix. Hanging plants will probably need daily watering; otherwise, keep the soil evenly moist. Water more frequently than other houseplants and mist daily. Light requirements vary. Ideally, a bright sunless window is best, but it thrives with less light. A bathroom spot where it gets illumination from a skylight or window, is good since it likes waves of warm humid air. Typical interior temperatures ranges are satisfactory. Feed twice a month through spring and summer with a complete fertilizer at half-strength.

Cissus antarctica

(SISS′us ant-ARD′tee-cuh)
Common Names: Vitis anarctica;
Kangaroo ivy; Kangaroo treevine
Nativity: Australia

One of the few plants that doesn't turn up its leaves at dim light, kangaroo ivy can be used to landscape a dark corner or other low-light areas. This virtue, combined with its tolerance of low humidity, make it a natural for apartments. Like its brother, *Cissus rhombifolia* (grape ivy), it's a vining climber which can be trained on a trellis, on wire, on a pole, or on virtually anything which its tendrils can anchor themselves to. The most attractive specimens are those whose growing tips have been pinched periodically through the spring. This promotes a thick, luxuriant growth and larger leaves. Plants treated in this manner are generally trained on stakes and kept under five feet, which is a chore since kangaroo ivy grows about as fast as anything in the plant kingdom. Characteristics of the plant are sawtoothed-edged leaves three to four inches long and almost as wide, and a weak vine which grows to ten

Cissus antarctica (Kangaroo Ivy)

feet, sometimes longer. A nice specimen can be created by potting up three or four young plants in a container. *C. antarctica* will produce an impressive display of foliage in a single growing season. **Price:** Potted kangaroos run from $1.49 for a single plant in a four-inch pot to $35 or more for a well-grown specimen several feet tall with five or six plants in the container. The best bargain in *C. antarctica* is canned stock which can often be found at the nursery under lath. Frequently, beautiful, full plants, six or more feet tall in five-gallon cans, are offered at the nursery for under $9. Try your local nursery in the spring.

Basic care: A basic soil mix kept slightly dry works best for *C. antarctica*. Let the soil dry out to a depth of two inches before irrigating again. Mist occasionally, or wipe the leaves with a moist paper towel, to remove dust and freshen. Although kangaroo ivy can survive in dim light, it prefers bright light or curtain-filtered sunlight, especially if the plant came from the lath house at the nursery. Can take direct sun in winter. While the traditional temperature recommendation for growing kangaroos is on the cool side—50° -

Cissus rhombifolia (Grape Ivy)

Codiaeum (Croton)

grape ivy, from its tendrils which make it a good climber, either up a trellis or bamboo stake. It also cascades nicely over the edge of a pot. If it is not pinched back occasionally, the stems get rather leggy, with widely-spaced leaves. These pinched-off stems can be rooted easily in water, then potted up to make more specimens. In fact, you should never have to buy more than one *C. rhombifolia*. Take care to see that the stems are not resting on moist topsoil since they have an annoying habit of rotting easily. **Price:** From 79¢ for a dish garden size up to $35 for a full potted specimen with several plants.

Basic care: Any good basic soil mix is suitable. Let the soil almost dry out before re-watering—a week to 10 days is usually sufficient in the typical interior environment. Medium light is best; a location in the middle of a room which gets average natural light is best, but it will tolerate very low light levels—say a corner with only artificial light. Normal interior temperatures are fine. It seems to respond to fish emulsion better than other fertilizers, but alternate with a chemical fertilizer and feed monthly spring to fall.

65°—my experience has been that the plant will take just about any night-day combination short of freezing or 100°+. Fertilizer doesn't seem to make much of an impression on the plant. It does as well with it as without it. Try feeding with a complete fertilizer diluted to half strength in April and July.

Cissus rhombifolia

(SISS'us rom-bih-FOAL'ee-uh)
Common Name: Grape ivy
Nativity: South America

This is one of the easiest and least expensive of all houseplants. It seems equally happy in a dimly-lit corner or bright sunless window. Continuous intense light causes the leaves to pale or yellow. Its leaves are almost rhomboidal in shape with sharp-toothed or serrated edges. It gets its common name,

Codiaeum

(co-dee-A'um)
Common Name: Croton
Nativity: Ceylon and Malaya

Although there are over 120 cultivars of *Codiaeum*, only as few as ten are currently available in the United States on a regular basis. First of all, you should know that crotons are extremely fussy plants which require continual care to thrive outside of the greenhouse. They frown on low humidity, cool drafts, too much sun in unventilated rooms and too little water. The high humidity requirement is the most difficult to fulfill. In its native habitat, the tropical air is full of moisture pretty much year round, and this environment can be duplicated in a hothouse. But, our homes fall far short of the humidity level needed. Frequent misting and

91

92

creation of a microclimate with a saucer filled with water-covered pebbles enhance your chances of success with this beautiful species. Like *Coleus*, crotons offer a wide range of foliage color accents and leaf shapes. Leaves may be oval or lance-shaped, twisted or curled. Leaves emerge green, then begin to take on tints of yellow, beige, orange, red, pink, and a dozen subtle, in-between shades. An unpruned plant can grow rapidly (one to two feet of height a year under ideal cultivation conditions) into a six-foot shrub. If you do head it back for height control, do so in early summer so the plant has time to recover before cool weather sets in and curtails growth. **Price:** Depending upon size, prices range from 89¢ to $25.

Basic care: Crotons favor a basic soil that is kept evenly moist, but never sopping wet or swampy. Plants situated in sunny locations in summer may need water every three days (in addition to frequent misting), while those grown in less intense light may require irrigation every six or seven days. A warmth lover, the ideal range is 65° at night and 80° during the day, but most adapt to higher temperature levels. Coolness isn't one of this plant's favorite things. Requires sun, winter and summer, to maintain brilliant foliage colors. Provide good cross-ventilation for those grown in sunny spots in summer. Most crotons willingly accept bright-to-medium light. Feed with a complete fertilizer diluted at half strength in May and again in July.

Coleus blumei

(COE'lee-us BLUE'my)
Common Name: Painted-leaf plant
Nativity: Asia

If you can provide bright, natural light, with even a little sun thrown in, *Coleus* is a colorful, trouble-free plant which takes to the indoors like a beaver to water. A native of the tropics, *Coleus* has been used primarily as a garden border or accent plant from New England to California and prized for its colorful

hues. Its striking color is what makes it desirable as a houseplant, particularly in winter, as it mimics floral hues ranging from red and orange to yellow and green. Propagation from cuttings and seeds is virtually foolproof and a packet of seeds will give you dozens of colorful variations. Leaves vary in length from about half an inch to four inches and maximum height is around four feet, depending upon the variety. The plant's natural tendency is to "go leggy"—dropping lower foliage. This can be frustrated by periodically pinching out the growing tips. This will keep *Coleus* bushy and full. Varieties with small leaves are good candidates for creating attractive hanging baskets. To save money, buy flats of *Coleus* from your local nursery, rather than potted plants. A flat should provide more than enough stock for two medium-sized or one large wire basket. *Coleus* does

Coleus

94

bloom outdoors, but only if it is situated in a partially-sunny window will it do so indoors. **Price:** Potted specimens from around 49¢ for a plant in a three-inch pot up to $25 and $30 for a well-grown plant shop specimen in a ten or twelve-inch container. Wire hanging baskets go for as little as $7.50 and as high as $25. Flats are usually offered for $4.00 to $7.00.

Basic care: Use a basic soil mix to which you add, if you wish, one tablespoon of ground limestone to a gallon of soil mix. The limestone isn't essential, but it helps. Keep the planting medium barely moist until late fall, then a little on the dry side until spring, but never let the soil completely dry out. The normal interior temperature ranges of 65° night and 75°-80° day are ideal for the plant. Some sun in summer, and maximum winter sun, keep the colors in the foliage vivid. *Coleus* will grow well in bright natural light, but foliage may dull somewhat. Feed every two weeks from spring to late fall with a complete fertilizer diluted to half strength. Watch for mealybugs on newly-acquired specimens. Since *Coleus* is sensitive to chemicals, you have to catch infestations early to control.

Cordyline stricta

(kor-dih-LIE'nee STRICK'tuh)
Common Name: Palm lily
Nativity: Australia

The *C. stricta* is often mistakenly sold as a dracaena, which it resembles and is closely related to, but it belongs to the lily family. Since it is sold in many areas of the country primarily as an outdoor accent plant, it is priced very reasonably, but this situation may change if a trend of using it indoors develops. Growers are quick to recognize such trends. *C. stricta* has a woody dracaena-like stalk (almost a trunk) and elongated leaf "blades" which measure ¾" by 8" long. As the plant matures, the lower leaves are sacrificed in favor of new top growth, creating a palm tree

Crassula argentea (Jade Tree)

effect. Mature specimens, which are often available at a moderate price, attain heights of eight and nine feet and usually require cutting back. This encourages new growth below the cuts, often in two or three places along the stem. **Price:** Generally available only in cans. Specimens in one-gallon cans run about $1.98 to $2.00; five-gallon cans, with several plants, fetch from $7.50 to $10. Occasionally one can find a really nice specimen eight or nine years old, six to seven feet tall, in a ten-gallon can, cloistered and forgotten in the back of a nursery. A find such as this should be costly, but it's not. I've seen them for as little as $12.95 to $14, but never higher than $16.

Basic care: Give *C. stricta* a basic soil mix kept barely moist. Mist occasionally to discourage spider mite and to raise the humidity. Can take some sun, but a window with

Cycas revoluta (Sago Palm)

trunk and branch structure and produces small, oval, jade-colored leaves which are tinged with red around the perimeter. Very old specimens often grow to four feet high and almost as wide. On rare occasions, a specimen which has received ideal treatment will produce clusters of pink flowers from about October to spring, but this usually only occurs when the plant is growing outdoors. Since it is a shallow-rooted plant, it may need some staking if the foliage gets top-heavy. *C. argentea* fanciers usually prune out wandering branches to keep the plant symmetrical. These, along with individual leaves, can be rooted in sand to create new plants. Don't bury the rooted branches; just the roots. When repotting, take care to maintain the previous soil level against the trunk. If the soil level is higher, the trunk may rot. **Price:** Dish garden specimens in 2″ pots, 59¢ to 89¢. Average prices for larger potted plants as follows: 4″-pot, $2.50; 6″-pot, $5.00; 8″-pot, $8.95. Older specimens, which may be in relatively small pots, are priced much higher.

Basic care: *Crassula argentea*, like most succulents which are water-storing plants, prefers a soil mix heavy on the sand for rapid drainage, but with some organic material. If the plant is in a sunny window, water as you would other houseplants; otherwise, let the soil become almost dry between waterings. If it is not getting sufficient moisture, its leaves will begin to wrinkle and drop. In this event, increase the frequency of irrigation. Full summer and winter sun. If this is not possible, then place the plant in the brightest spot in the room. High temperatures suit it fine, as do cooler nighttime ranges. Feed in April and June with a complete fertilizer at full strength.

filtered sun is preferable. Will survive with less illumination. The typical interior temperature range is quite satisfactory. Feed monthly or bimonthly with fish emulsion, and alternate with a chemical fertilizer. Mealybug infestation is a frequent pest problem with *C. stricta*. Look for them deep in the crevices where the leaves join the stem and remove them with a cotton swab dipped in alcohol.

Crassula argentea
(KRASS'uh-luh   ar-GEN'tee-uh)
Common Names: Jade tree;
Chinese rubber plant
Nativity: Primarily South Africa

Long a favorite for the succulent dish garden, *C. argentea* is now gaining popularity as a large, easy-maintenance houseplant. It resembles a miniature tree with its thick, fleshy

Cycas revoluta
(SY'cus   rev-o-LUTE'uh)
Common Name: Sago palm
Nativity: Asia, particularly Japan

If this plant looks like a holdover from the

age of the dinosaur, it's because it *is* very primitive. It is not really a palm; it's a cycad (SY'kad) in the *Cycadaceae* (sik-uh-DAY' see-ee) family which goes back to the dawn of botanical history. It *does* resemble a palm with its stiff fronds which carry thin, pinnately-divided evergreen leaves emanating in rosette fashion from a stout trunk. It is a slow-grower and the more mature a specimen is, the higher the price. **Price:** In one-gallon cans, $4.95 to $6.95; in five-gallon cans, $20 to $40. Mature potted specimens, about three feet across, average in price from $25 up to $50, but can go higher.

Basic care: Pot up in a rich, basic soil mix. Water thoroughly when the soil is dry one inch below surface. Plant benefits from a period of drought between waterings. Likes a window with filtered sun, but appreciates full winter sun. Will grow with artificial light, but prefers the higher intensity of natural illumination. Suited to normal interior temperatures. Feed monthly with a complete fertilizer at half-strength during spring and summer.

Dieffenbachia
(diff-in-BACK'ee-uh)
Common Names: Dumb cane;
Mother-in-Law's tongue
Nativity: Primarily South America

Another perennial American favorite, but only three or four of the 30 varieties are commonly available. Like the *Ficus decora*, it is hardy and takes a great deal of abuse before quitting. The two most popular species, which seem to adapt well to most households, are *D. amoena* and *D. picta*. *D. amoena* seems hardier than most and is the species usually stocked by most plant outlets. It can take a temperature dip down to a chilly 45°, which is frowned upon by most other tropicals, but it doesn't like cold drafts. It's a fast-grower, and produces deep to medium-green leaves splotched with cream markings, from about 8″ to 20″ long, emanating from a thick

green stem, or trunk, *D. picta* prefers more tropical temperatures. The most striking of the *picta* species is the Rudolph Roehrs, which has light green leaves and either cream or yellow markings. Most *Dieffenbachias* I've grown and seen others grow have an annoying habit of trading off the lowest leaf everytime a new one develops so that, in time, one has an enormous serpentine trunk with an insignificant burst of foliage at the very top. Pinching out new growth when the plant is young has no effect—it still sacrifices the oldest leaf, so that about every second year you must air layer and start all over. The sap of *Dieffenbachia* is toxic and can cause temporary speech loss and irritation or swelling of the mucous membranes of the mouth and throat. Obviously, if one has small children or a gnawing puppy, this might not be the best plant choice. **Price:** Available almost

Dieffenbachia picta (Dumbcane)

everywhere in 6″ pots (about two feet tall) for $3.95 to $5.95. Four to five-footers should sell for about $8 to $10. Really showy specimens are generally priced from $40 up to $85.

Basic care: Does well in a basic planting medium kept on the dry side. *Dieffenbachias* are definitely not sun-worshipers, although they may tolerate winter sun. Medium-bright illumination is best, five to six feet back from a north exposure window. I have seen specimens doing well in homes with only artificial illumination. Normal household temperature ranges are adequate. Feed monthly from spring to fall with a complete fertilizer at half-strength.

Dizygotheca elegantissima

(dizzy-goth-EEK′kuh el-ee-gan-TISS′ee-muh)
Common Names: Aralia elegantissima;
False aralia
Nativity: South Pacific

This native of New Caledonia is often sold as the "marijuana plant" because of the resemblance its serrated, palmate leaves have to the *Cannabis*, or marijuana, plant. It is one of those tricky specimens, like the so-called Boston fern, which is difficult for many novices to grow successfully. One must strike on (then maintain) the exact soil aridity-moisture relationship. If the soil is too dry or too wet, it will "throw" its foliage. As it matures, it drops its lower leaves and attains a tree-like appearance. Actually, it is a tree, growing to heights of 15 to 20 feet in its native habitat (and even in Florida and California). It's a good candidate for both air layering (in early spring) and bonsai gardens.
Price: A specimen in a 2″ pot fetches around 89¢; a one-footer should go for $1.98 to $2.95; three-footers usually bring $5 to $8.50; after that, add about $10 a foot.

Basic care: Prefers a basic soil mix that drains well. Keep the soil evenly moist and friable. Favors a bright window with filtered sun, but can take full winter sun. It will grow

Dracaena massangeana (Corn Plant)

in less light, but does not fare well with only artificial illumination, unless it has a special flourescent set-up for indoor gardening. Normal interior temperatures are adequate. Feed monthly from spring to fall with a complete fertilizer at half-strength. Watch it carefully for scale infestation. Scale seem very fond of *Dizygothecas*.

Dracaena fragrans massangeana

(druh-SEEN′uh FRAY′grons
mass-ON′gee-on-uh)
Common Name: Corn plant
Nativity: South Pacific

Although Massange's dracaena is commonly called the corn plant, it's priced like strawberries in mid-winter, being one of the more expensive of the exotics. Its common designation comes from the characteristics of the foliage—long, slightly turned-under

leaves usually about three-feet long and 3" to 4" wide, accented with a pale green or yellow stripe down the center, quite similar to corn. The foliage is carried on stout fawn-colored stalks, or trunks, which in maturity reach heights of six and seven feet. Although not well-known as a houseplant among novice collectors, it has been a favorite of architects and designers for plush interiors for a number of years because of its striking appearance and ability to adjust and do magnificently in almost any environment. **Price:** Specimens in a one-gallon can or six-inch pot (about 16" tall) are priced usually not lower than $10 but often as high as $20; two plants in a pot or a single plant two feet tall, $35 to $45. Very showy specimens, with four to six plants of staggered heights from two- to six-feet tall, run between $175 to $250, although I've seen such specimens outdoors (under lath) at California nurseries in ten-gallon cans for as low as $100. Usually, there is some foliar damage evident in such "finds" from sun, wind, and careless handling, but this can be trimmed and will be replaced by the plant in time.

Basic Care: A standard "basic" soil mix is suitable, kept evenly moist. Water more frequently than other houseplants. Although it survives in low-light conditions, it really takes off in bright natural light, such as a north window or three to four feet back from a curtain-draped west window. It likes all the winter sun it can get, but summer sun scorches its foliage. Typical interior temperature ranges are satisfactory. Mist occasionally, though, to moisten up hot, dry air in summer and to keep the leaves dust-free. Feed bi-monthly from early spring to early fall with a complete fertilizer at half-strength. Common pests which afflict this species are mites, mealybugs and scale.

Dracaena warneckii

Dracaena marginata
(druh-SEEN'uh mar-juh-NOT'uh)
Common Names: Dragon tree; Madagascar dragon tree
Nativity: Madagascar

Of the several varieties available, the *D. marginata* is the most sought after and, alas, often the costliest. It is most attractive when several plants of varying heights are potted up in one container. The trunk, which is palm-like in appearance, has a delightful tendency to twist and turn as it grows (up to nine feet tall), carrying at its branch tips rosettes of sword-like, olive-colored leaves edged with red. It is extremely slow growing, which is one factor that governs its high price—it can't be cultivated rapidly, even in the greenhouse. A specimen six-feet tall, for example, is usually about eight to ten years old. **Price:** Even the smallest specimen, when available, is a bit high-priced compared with other plants of similar size. Most growers deliver *marginatas* in 5" or 6" pots (8" to 12" specimens) which are priced at $6 to $8. Prices skyrocket from here to as much as $250 for a container with five or six plants of varying heights. An average price for three plants in a pot 18″ to 24″ tall is $45.

Basic care: Standard soil mix kept evenly moist. A bright but sunless window is ideal, but a spot near a window (four to five feet back) or under a skylight is satisfactory. Normal (comfortable) interior temperatures are adequate, but a warm humid environment is best. Feed monthly from spring to fall with a complete fertilizer at half-strength. The *Dracaena marginata* is a favorite target of spider mites, and sometimes scale and mealybugs try to move in. If some mishap befalls the foliage, you can cut back the trunk to about the rim level of the pot and, provided the roots are undamaged, the plant will "stump-sprout."

Dracaena warneckii
(druh-SEEN'uh WAR'nek-ee)
Common Name: Stripe-leafed dracaena
Nativity: Africa

Not enough can be said in praise of this hardy, durable and beautiful plant. It is one of the least fussy of all the plants one could select for indoor cultivation. Although it prefers medium bright light, it adapts to partial sun, yet it settles in nicely in a fairly dim corner. It has the classic dracaena characteristics—upright stem and long, sword-like leaves. *D. warneckii* is distinctive in that its leaves, which average sixteen inches in length, are deep green and either striped or edged in white. It is a relatively slow grower, adding about four to six inches yearly in a typical home environment. It does attain impressive height with maturity—about 10 feet at 10 years. It can stand some neglect. Dust on the leaves doesn't seem to thwart it and it weathers periods of drought quite well. Plants four to five years old may throw suckers and damaged plants that are cut back often branch to produce an attractive tree-like specimen. In temperate climates you can find

the plant under lath at the nursery from time to time. These adapt with ease and are usually a genuine bargain. **Price:** Available as a dish garden plant almost everywhere for about 69¢. Specimens eight to ten inches tall in four inch pots are reasonable at $1.98 to $3.95. A nice "showcase" set-up, three plants of staggered heights in a twelve-inch container, is generally ticketed for around $30 but can go as high as $60.

Basic care: *D. warneckii* flourishes in a basic soil mix and, although it prefers to have the soil just barely moist, it will tolerate dry spells. Too much and too frequent watering, however, browns off leaves. It prefers medium natural light, but does very nicely on only artificial illumination. It survives in very bright or very dim conditions, so one should be able to adapt it to virtually any interior location short of full summer sun or total darkness. Average interior temperatures ranges are suitable, and cooler-than-normal levels are acceptable, provided the mercury

Euphorbia hermentiana (African Milk Tree)

Fatsia japonica (Japanese Aralia)

remains above 50°. Feed monthly from April to September with a complete fertilizer at half-strength. Keep its roots crowded longer than most plants; it does better than many with "tight shoes."

Euphorbia
(you-FOR'bee-uh)
Common Names: (See below)
Nativity: Primarily Africa

Most members of the *Euphorbia* family are succulents and some closely resemble cacti. Two oddities in the family are *E. pulcherrima*, or poinsettia, and *E. millii*, or *E. splendens*, commonly called "Crown of Thorns." Of the more than 1,600 species, only a few have been cultivated indoors, although many more could be successfully grown in sunny windows. Some favorites are: *E. biglandulosa*, which grows to two feet with few branches, and produces grayish-green leaves about 1½ inches long. It blooms in winter or early spring with a yellow bract.
E. caerulescens, a shrub which may attain five feet and produces four to five angled branches and half-inch spines.
E. canariensis, which becomes a 20-ft. tree outdoors but can be kept indoors for years as a juvenile. It has thick angled branches and black spines.
E. lactea, or "milk striped Euphorbia," which grows upright dark-green angled stems with a marbled white band down the center. The plant resembles a candelabra in form. A cultivar, *E. lactea cristata*, often called "Elkhorn" or "Frilled fan," is an unusual specimen with crested, frilly branches.
E. trigona, or *hermentiana* (illustrated), commonly called the African milk tree, is a durable plant which produces erect, spiny, crested branches.

The milky sap of most *Euphorbia* species is both poisonous and can irritate sensitive skin. On the plus side, most need very little care and, if conditions are right, produce colorful blooms seasonally. **Price:** Depending, as always, upon size, you can expect to pay as little as 89¢ for the smallest of specimens up to about $10 for a good-sized plant. Best buys are found in cans at the nursery.

Basic care: A basic soil mix with some additional horticultural charcoal (crushed) and one tablespoon of limestone to a gallon of mix produces the best results. Remember that *Euphorbias* are succulent, so keep the planting medium on the dry side by letting it dry out to a depth of two inches before irrigating again. Most prefer curtain-filtered sunlight, but if the plant seems to be deteriorating, give it full sun for two or three hours a day. Some may survive on bright natural light, but dimmer illumination is usually insufficient. The warm temperature range of 65° to 80° is ideal. Feed with a complete fertilizer at full strength once a year, in early spring.

103

104

Fatsia japonica

(FAT'see-uh juh-PON'ih-kuh)
Common Names: Aralia sieboldii;
Japanese aralia
Nativity: Japan

F. japonica makes an attractive showy houseplant with its dense foliage mass of leathery, palmately-lobed, dark-green leaves and, in winter, its long panicles of white flowers. (For larger leaf development, the flowers should be snipped off as they develop.) It has a trunky stem, much like that of the Schefflera, but, unlike the Schefflera, its stem often twists, turns and distorts itself, creating a striking effect. F. japonica will let you know when it's dehydrated by allowing its branches to droop, which frequently happens during hot spells or in an overheated unventilated interior environment. It propagates well from either cuttings or suckers near the soil line. **Price:** Specimens in one-gallon cans can usually be obtained for 98¢ to $1.98; those in five-gallon cans at $4.95 to $8.95. Potted plants range from $5.95 to $35, depending upon size and the number of plants in the container.

Basic care: Does best in a fast-draining, basic soil mix kept friable and almost damp. Suffers some in full summer sun, but can take winter sun. Ideally, a position in or near a bright window is best, but it will survive with less illumination. It seems to like cooler temperatures than most houseplants and flags in overheated (80°+) interiors. Daily misting and setting the plant on a dry well of water-covered pebbles helps it contend with heat waves. Feed with a complete fertilizer at half-strength monthly from early spring through late fall.

Ficus benjamina

(FY'cus ben-juh-MEEN'uh)
Common Names: Weeping fig; Weeping Chinese banyan; Benjamin tree
Nativity: India

Highly prized for its elegant appearance, easy maintenance and evergreen quality. It belongs to the same family as the F. elastica (rubber tree) and F. lyrata (fiddleleaf fig) but is rarely available in many areas of the country, and then only limited quantities. Native to India, it is classified as semi-tropical and likes sunny humid conditions. In its native habitat it can grow to 35 feet, but indoors, seven to eight feet is average. Selective pruning keeps it manageable indoors. Its glossy leaves and drooping branch structure (from whence it gets its popular name) emanating from a tawny trunk, make it an attractive focal point for an entry, sunny corner or main window. If you want to keep a F. benjamina full, prune out new growth as it appears until you achieve the foliage density you want. This will also encourage branching. If you're after height, let the new growth thrive and prune lower branches. Make your cuts as

Ficus benjamina

close to the trunk as possible, using a single-edge razor blade. **Price:** Nurseries and plant shops charge extortionate prices for the hothouse-grown specimens, which are intended for interior use. A tree just three feet high goes for an average of $18 to $20; five to six-footers bring from $30 to as much as $125, with an average of $85. If you are fortunate enough to live in a warmbelt area where the *F. benjamina* is field-grown for exterior use, you can acquire a fine specimen very reasonably and adapt it to survive indoors. Field-grown *F. benjaminas* are priced at about $15 to $25 for a five-footer in a five-gallon can.

Basic care: A standard, organically-rich soil mix kept barely moist is best. Your watering schedule will vary, depending on where you keep the plant. If it's in the sun for a few hours each day, you may have to water twice a week. If it's in a corner or entry, it may require water only once every eight to ten days. A daily misting is beneficial, but not vital to clear the stomata of dust and raise the humidity level. Adapts well to the typical household temperature level. Location is important. The *F. benjamina* is one of the few houseplants which can take direct sun through a window. If you have a window which gets dappled sunlight for a few hours each day (east or west window, usually), this is best. Second choice is very bright natural light all day (north exposure). It will survive in poorer illumination, and I have seen beautiful specimens whose only source of light was a draped window or artificial illumination. Feed monthly from April through September with a complete fertilizer at half-strength. Scale are fond of *benjaminas*.

Ficus elastica decora
(FY′cus ee-LASS′tee-kuh deh-CORE′uh)
Common Name: Rubber tree, or rubber plant
Nativity: India and Malaya

This is one of the two most popular houseplants in America—the other, of course, being the ubiquitous *Monstera deliciosa*, or split-leaf philodendron. It has survived over the years as a household favorite because it is virtually indestructible. It takes in stride both overwatering and underwatering and is virtually disease and insect-free, although scale sometimes are a problem. I've seen *F. decora* growing well in dark corners and sunny windows. The original strain came from India where it attained heights of 30 feet and more. Its dark green, leathery oval leaves which, at maturity, are five to 10 inches long and four to six inches across, grow from a red sheath which turns brown and usually drops off. If this sheath fails to drop, it should be removed by hand or it may cause the new leaf to rot. One of the primary objections many people have to the *F. decora* is that it soon becomes leggy by dropping its lower leaves as new foliage emerges. To some extent, this is a natural phenomenon, but overwatering can

Ficus lyrata

hasten the process. One technique which sometimes encourages branching and/or retention of lower leaves is pinching out the new leaves at the growing tip before they open. An alternative is to air layer the plant and start again. Because *F. decora* has a tendency to become leggy, it is always a good idea to pot up three plants in one pot. As they grow together, the foliage mass gives the appearance of a single, lush, full specimen. **Price:** Because of almost universal availability, the *F. decora* is relatively inexpensive. Average prices run from $1.29 to $1.75 for a one-footer in a 4″ pot and $3.95 to $4.50 for a plant two- to three-feet tall in a 6″ pot. Really nice specimens, from five- to six-feet tall with two or three plants in the pot, usually bring $35 to $70. I've seen them priced higher, but felt because of their widespread availability and easy cultivation, they were overpriced.

Ficus lyrata (Fiddle-Leaf Fig)

Basic care: A rich, general-purpose soil mix is best and it should be kept barely moist. While *F. decora* seems to like a bright sunless window best, it will thrive in a completely windowless environment with only limited artificial light, although its growth will be slower. It's not finicky about temperature levels. If a room is comfortable for you, it will be acceptable to your *F. decora*. It isn't, however, fond of cold drafts or frigid conditions, but copes well with an air-conditioned environment. Wash off its leaves from time to time with Ivory soap and follow with a clear-water rinse. You may use leaf polish to enhance the glossiness of the leaves and eliminate hard water stains, provided the label states that the product is non-toxic. From early spring to late fall feed bi-monthly with a complete fertilizer, such as fish emulsion, diluted to half-strength.

Ficus lyrata

(FY′cus lie-ROT′uh)
Common Names: Ficus pandurata;
Fiddleleaf fig
Nativity: Africa

This highly-desirable tropical is one of the scarce specimens which is often priced out of sight. In its native habitat or under ideal greenhouse conditions, it has unlimited growth potential, attaining heights of 100 feet and more. Its beautiful, glistening, fiddle-shaped leaves grow to 18″ and 20″ in length and nearly as wide, and make it a favorite interior accent plant among architects and decorators. You can train the plant to conform to almost any space by tying down the stem. Use a gentle touch, since too much pressure may snap it in two. To force branching, pinch out new growth when plant is young. **Price:** Since the *F. lyrata* is always in demand, it is dearly priced. A specimen two-feet tall usually goes for $10 to $15— sometimes $20. Larger specimens average about $10 a foot, depending upon how many plants are in the container.

Ficus retusa nitida (Indian Laurel)

Basic care: Like most tropicals, the *F. lyrata* thrives in a rich organic soil mix kept moist. Bright diffuse light is best. It can take full winter sun or it will adjust to minimal artificial illumination, although not quite so little as the *F. decora* can get by on. Temperature levels in the 55° to 80° range are suitable. Because of the wide leaf surfaces, dust is a continual problem. Wipe them once a week with a damp paper towel or cloth. From early spring to late fall feed monthly with a complete fertilizer at half-strength.

Ficus retusa nitida

(FY′cus ruh-TOO′suh NIT′ih-duh)
Common Name: Indian laurel
Nativity: Indian and Malaya

An obscure but nonetheless desirable, easy to grow and handsome fig family member that attains heights indoors of six to seven feet. Its leaves are oval, deep green and average 3½″ long and ¾″ to an inch wide. Its branch structure tends to be erratic if not pruned and shaped periodically, but this effect may not be undesirable. **Price:** When available, most nurseries sell in cans $4.95 to $6.95 for a one-gallon specimen; $8.95 to $10.95 for *F. nitidas* in five-gallon cans. Potted mature specimens are priced anywhere from $50 to $125, depending upon the outlet.

Basic care: Pot up in an organically-rich soil mix kept barely moist. Let topsoil go dry to a depth of an inch before watering. Prefers bright diffuse natural light (a north exposure), but can take a few hours of sun (full winter sun). Will also survive in good artificial illumination. Adjusts well to normal interior temperatures but likes the humidity raised periodically. The leaves show dust easily and need wiping with a damp cloth once a week. From spring to fall feed monthly with a complete fertilizer at half-strength.

Howeia belmoreana

(HOW′ee-uh bell-mor-ee-AHN′uh)
Also called Kentia belmoreana
Common Names: Kentia palm; Sentry palm
Nativity: Lord Howe Island, South Pacific

A classic of the indoor plant world, the often maligned sentry palm is still a highly-desirable and expensive houseplant. Its elegant branches grow from trunks ringed with the scars of pruned-out leaves. Its natural tendency is to spread, but lashing the fronds together keeps it confined to a given space. Once deprecated as the cliché plant for hotel lobbies, this native of Lord Howe Island in the South Pacific is currently enjoying a resurgence of popularity, which is reflected in rising prices. It takes an amazing amount of abuse—heat, drafts, dust, drought—and continues to plod along, adding about seven inches of growth a year under ideal environmental conditions. Don't be overzealous about repotting; it does well for years in its original container. **Price:** When available

110

Howeia belmoreana (Kentia Palm)

from nurseries, they are usually offered in two-gallon and five-gallon cans, about three and five feet high, respectively. The former are priced a rather exorbitant $25 to $35; the latter easily bring $50 to $80, and—if potted up—$125 to $150 is not uncommon.

Basic care: Soil should be a basic mix kept evenly moist. Bright, natural illumination seems to produce the best results and a typical interior temperature range suits its needs. Feed monthly with a complete fertilizer diluted to half-strength from early spring to late summer. All of the foregoing are ideal conditions. Sentry palms can survive in dark corners without much water for long periods. For this reason, they're perfect for neglectful indoor gardeners. They are, however, prone to scale infestation, so check for this every two weeks, especially in the spring.

Medinilla magnifica
(med-in-ILL'uh mag-NIF'ih-kuh)
Common Name: Rose grape
Nativity: Philippines; Java

Once thought to be suitable only as a greenhouse resident, M. magnifica has moved indoors to adorn the homes of those gardeners who are willing to give the plant the additional care it needs to thrive. And, what it needs to thrive is high humidity —60% to 70%, which means a microclimate and frequent misting through the spring and summer months. If you're willing to devote the extra time, you'll get a beautiful specimen which lives up to its name by throwing a long panicle of red blooms with purple anthers, topped by large pink bracts. Blooming occurs only on mature plants and flowers can appear any time, but it's most likely they'll appear in spring and summer. The foliage itself is attractive—thick, leathery dark-green leaves which grow in pairs along branching stems. Eventually, the plant will reach five feet. Don't be in a hurry to pot on; M. magnifica does best if left in the same container two or three years. Give the plant a rest from about November to February by cutting back on water and moving the plant to dimmer illumination. This will encourage more spectacular growth in the coming year. Since the plant is rarely found, at this writing, except in specialty plant shops, you may want to propagate by rooting cuttings in milled peat moss and sand. Other family members which are not as impressive as M. magnifica but may adapt as easily are M. amabilis, also called M. teysmannii, and M. curtisi. **Price:** When available, a specimen may be tagged from $15 to $35, depending upon size. Because of the relative rarity of the plant, there is no price structure, *per se*.

Basic care: The plant seems to do best in a special medium which is marketed as "orchid mix." This should be kept evenly moist until November, then on the dry side until March. Misting and other provisions for high humidity should continue from spring to fall.

112

A spot that gets sun filtered through a thin curtain is the first place to try *M. magnifica*. Second choice should be a bright natural light window or nearby. Keep the plant warm—65°-80°. Feed in March, May and July with a complete fertilizer diluted to half strength.

Monstera deliciosa

(mon-STIR'uh   del-ih-see-OH'suh)
Also called Philodendron pertusum
Common Names: Split-leaf philly;
Swiss cheese plant; Mexican breadfruit
Nativity: Mexico and Central America

Ranks with the "rubber tree" as the most universally collected plant in America because of its easy availability, moderate price, tolerance of improper treatment and hot, dry household environments. A Central American native, the *Monstera deliciosa* grows to fantastic heights and produces cone-like edible fruit which tastes like both pineapple and banana, in its natural environment. The best one can hope for in the average living room conditions is, perhaps, ten feet of height. Much of its appeal is in characteristics of its glossy, deeply-lobed dark green leaves which often grow to 12″ and 13″ long and almost as wide. Most novice indoor gardeners who own a *M. deliciosa* have long since become disenchanted with it. What was once a beautiful, full specimen is now a thick, naked stalk trailing strange, serpentine cords and, perhaps, crowned with a few stunted, misshapen leaves. *Deliciosas* are vining plants and, left to their own devices, get leggy. The secret is to start pinching out all new growth the moment you acquire the plant and continue to do so for the next three to four months. It's difficult to do—sacrificing all those new green leaves—but this will cause the rest of the foliage to fill out, giving you a thick, luxuriant specimen. Let the plant go for about two months, then resume pinching back for a while. If you continue to do this for a year or more, the result will be well worth your orig-

inal anguish. The "ropes" which hang down are aerial roots and should be placed in the pot where they will anchor in the soil to carry food up to the plant, or affixed to the moss stake with green twist-ties where they will attach themselves, if the moss is kept moist, and help support the plant. Always water the stake thoroughly when you irrigate the plant. **Price:** Easily affordable in the smaller sizes: $3.50 to $5.95 for a three-foot plant in a 6″ pot. Larger specimens, already potted up, about five-feet tall are generally available for $12 to $18.

Basic care: Favors a basic soil mix kept just barely moist. Needs daily misting, but this is not vital to its survival. Keep its moss stake moist. A bright, filtered-sun window location

Monstera deliciosa

Monstera deliciosa (Split-Leaf Philodendron)

or nearby is preferred, but almost any spot, whether illuminated by natural or artificial light, will do. If the light level is inadequate, new leaves will be smaller and not so well-formed. This should be your cue to move the plant closer to a light source. Adapts well to typical household temperatures and is tolerant of cooler (50° and hotter 85°+) levels. Feed monthly from early spring to fall with a complete fertilizer at half-strength. If you have a specimen that has deteriorated into a barren stalk, you can propagate by cutting the stem into pieces about six inches long and rooting them in a mixture of 50% sand and 50% leaf mold. Keep the cuttings in a warm place covered with plastic wrap until they root, then pot up. Poke a couple of holes in the plastic wrap to keep the soil from souring or mold from forming.

Nephrolepsis exaltata bostoniensis
(Boston Fern)

Nephrolepsis exaltata
(neh-FROL'ep-sis ex-all-TOT'uh)
Common Names: Sword fern; Boston fern
(*N. exaltata bostoniensis*)
Nativity: South America, Africa, Asia

Great-grandmother's Victorian favorite, the "Boston fern," is making a strong comeback after having fallen into disfavor as being "old fashioned." Few people are successful with ferns and, particularly, this species, although fern fanciers aver it is one of the best-suited for interior culture. Inevitably, for most beginners, the fronds brown off and the plant thins out pitifully, in most cases. The reason: *N. exalta* must have bright, diffuse light (but no sun) and high humidity—much higher than most other houseplants. It does not do as well as a hanging plant because of the rising hot dry air. Its characteristics are arching pinnate fronds which grow 18″ to 24″ long and 3″ to 6″ broad, carrying compactly-set leaves 3″ long. It propagates itself by spore production (in its natural habitat) and by sending out creeping rhizomes (RY'zomes), or stems, which root and produce new plants. These can be removed and potted up to increase your stock. **Price:** Usually available potted-up in plastic containers as follows: 4″-pot, $3.95 to $4.95; 6″-pot, $6.95 to $8.50; 7″ to 8″ pots, $10 to $15.

Basic care: Seems to prefer a mix of peat moss and sandy soil, kept on the moist side, over any other medium. Water daily or every other day. Must have bright diffuse natural light and no summer sun, but give it full winter sun. Needs cooler temperatures than most houseplants—around 50° at night and not above 75° during the day. Erratic temperature fluctuations during the day or night are not good for this fern. If the interior temperature is consistently higher than 75° during the day, and during heat waves, mist two or three times a day. Likes fish emulsion every two months from early spring to fall, at half-strength. Common pests which have an affinity for ferns are aphids, mealybugs and scale. Check the plant regularly since infestation is difficult to eradicate in a full, bushy specimen. Don't mistake those regularly-spaced black specks which may develop under the leaves for scale infestation. These are spore casings which, if the plant is growing wild, are the primary method of propagation of the species.

Ornithogalum
(or-nih-THOG'ul-um)
Common Names: False sea onion;
Healing onion
Nativity: Primarily South Africa

Another oddity of the plant kingdom, false sea onions are bulbous herbs of the Lily family which produce often striking, fragrant flowers which last for days in vases, and all make excellent indoor (or outdoor, in mild climates) container plants. Some varieties have been used in the past as folk medicine remedies for colds and bruises. Their common name—false sea onion—is a natural since they closely resemble an overgrown onion (see illustration). Four that do well indoors are:

O. arabicum (ar-AB'ih-cum). Grows to two feet and produces leaves about the same length. Fragrant blooms are one-inch-long, white, with a glossy black pistil.

O. caudatum (caw-DOT'um) Attains three feet of height with curling leaves up to two feet long. Flowers are small, star-shaped, white and striped green.

O. narbonense (nar-bon-ENTS') Grows to about two feet with leaves nearly as long. White and green accented flowers are two inches wide.

O. saundersiae (SAWN'der-say) Striking plant with leaves up to one-and-a-half feet long and stalks five feet tall which carry many white flowers with glossy, greenish-black pistils.

The general cultivation practice is to allow bulbs to go dormant naturally after blooming and store them in their container in a cellar, cabinet under the sink or other dark, cool spot until October, then knock them out and repot them in virgin soil in the same container, which has been scrubbed and dried. Bulbs purchased at the nursery or plant shop should be planted three or four to a pot to create a nice floral-foliage display in spring and summer. **Price:** Available almost everywhere from $1.95 for one potted bulb to about $10 for a container with several bulbs.

Basic care: Does well in a basic soil mix kept evenly moist during the growing season, then on the dry side. Most prefer direct sun for three or four hours a day, but a location that gets curtain-filtered sunlight probably will work just as well. Not too fussy about temperature levels. Adjusts to the typical indoor ranges. Feed monthly from April to August with a complete fertilizer at half strength.

Ornithogalum caudatum (False Sea Onion)

Phildodendron selloum
(fill-oh-DEN'drun suh-LOOM')
Common Names: Tree philodendron; saddle-leaf philodendron
Nativity: South America

One of the few "self-heading" philodendrons, which means its branch structure emanates from a trunk. Most philodendrons are vining. *P. selloum* closely resembles *Monstera deliciosa* (split-leaf philodendron) when it is young. As it matures, its leaves become deeply lobed and eventually grow from twelve to twenty inches long and ten to fourteen inches wide. Damaged foliage can be cut off at the trunk and will soon be replaced with new leaves with a lighter green color that deepens into emerald green at maturity. The leaves unfurl from a sheath which browns off and should be removed if it doesn't drop off. *P. selloum* is a "spreader" and, if grown under optimum conditions, will attempt to take over a room. In temperate areas of the country, this is one of the least expensive plants to acquire. Nursery lath houses are always loaded with beautiful specimens in one and five-gallon cans. Three plants from one-gallon cans may be potted together in about a twelve-inch container to create an impressive display of foliage. If this is done, say, in April, by July the plant will have taken over an entire corner. If too much space is being invaded, the leaves can be lashed together or selectively pruned out. **Price:** In one-gallon cans, $1.98 to $2.50; in five-gallon cans, $5.95 to $8.50. Potted specimens are slightly higher.

Basic care: Needs a basic soil mix kept barely moist. Needs daily misting in winter. A bright window location that admits curtain-filtered sunlight produces the best-looking plants, but most adapt to north or south window exposures. Interior temperature levels which suit it best are in the 55°-80° range. Feed monthly from early spring to fall with a complete fertilizer at half-strength.

Phoenix roebelenii (Pigmy Date Palm)

Phoenix roebelenii
(FEE'nix roe-bul-EE'nee)
Common Names: Pigmy date palm; Dwarf date palm
Nativity: Asia, particularly Burma

Since its importation from China in the late 19th Century, *P. roebelenii* has been the most popular palm for indoor cultivation, after the *Kentia*. Like the *Kentia*, *P. roebelenii* is durable, easily cared for, slow-growing, and adapts easily to most interior environments. As a dwarf, it will not make any future space demands. Most average only two feet; some reach five feet after several years, and very old, well-grown specimens may attain six feet, but this is exceedingly rare indoors. Characteristics are arching, feathery fronds which grow from a typical palm trunk to one or two feet in length and are covered with

Podocarpus nagi
(Japanese Yew)

compactly-set leaflets about six inches long. Mature specimens may develop suckers at the soil line and these may be removed, to concentrate growth energy to a single trunk, or left to develop. It's a matter of personal taste. Plants purchased already potted up will not need potting on for several years. Those bought in cans should be potted into a container soon after purchase. New soil must be jammed tightly into the pot to achieve what is called a "hard pack." The plant grows much better if the soil is pressing firmly against its roots. **Price:** Specimens already potted in terra cotta containers are generally priced according to size. The smallest, often dish garden size, may sell for as little as $1 or under. The largest, which will probably be around two feet high with an equal foliage spread, may command the princely sum of $50

—maybe more—but, average pigmy palms should go for around $10. Canned palms at the nursery are more reasonable—$2.50 for one in a gallon can; $7.50 and up for one in a five-gallon can.

Basic care: Most do best in a basic soil mix with an extra trowel of sand, to promote efficient drainage. During spring and summer, keep the soil evenly moist, but never wet or boggy. In fall and winter, let the soil dry out to a depth of an inch before watering again. Humidity requirements are slightly higher than for many houseplants. Mist or wipe the fronds with a damp cloth daily in hot weather. A microclimate created by a saucer of water-covered pebbles under the plant helps keep the leaflet tips green and healthy. Light is important in the cultivation of pigmy palms. The first choice, from the plant's point-of-view, in or near a window which admits curtain-filtered sunlight. Second choice is a spot that gets bright natural light. Dimly-lit corners spell doom for this species. Temperature preferences are on the warm side—65° at night and 80° during the day, but most adapt to normal household levels. However, the plant may deteriorate in cool environments. Feed monthly from April through July with a complete fertilizer at half strength.

Podocarpus

(poe-doe-CAR′pus)
Common Names (Many)
Nativity: Primarily Africa and Japan

Of the four primary varieties available in this country, the *P. maki* seems easiest to adapt to an interior environment, although the *P. nagi*, or Japanese podocarpus, does quite well indoors. They are members of the Yew family and are native to Asia, Africa, Australia and South America. This is one plant (a tree, actually) which not only can withstand direct sun, but needs it to really thrive. Its dark green leaves which resemble flat needles lose color and yellow off in dim light. The *P. maki* eventually makes a main focal point specimen reaching seven feet in height if left unpruned, and becomes shrubbier if cut back at the growing tips. If you have high ceilings, and want a real tree, choose the *P. magi*, since it grows much taller. You can propagate from stem cuttings. **Price:** Sometimes available in one-gallon cans at $1.89 to $2.50 and five-gallon cans for $6.95 to $8.50. A potted specimen, four feet tall in a 6″ or 8″ pot, would be fairly priced at $10 to $15.

Basic care: *Podocarpus* likes a rich, coarse basic mix laced with sand for fast drainage. Allow the soil to dry out down to a depth of one inch before watering again, then saturate the soil. You must have a sunny window or skylight to keep a *Podocarpus* content indoors, although you may get by with a north window exposure. Interior temperatures are suitable and extremes are no problem. Both the *P. maki* and *P. nagi* are tolerant of cool environments (down to 40°, sometimes lower). Feed monthly with a complete fertilizer from spring to fall and, if you pot up from the can, sprinkle two tablespoons of steamed bonemeal over the bottom layer of soil.

Pseudopanax lessonii
(sue-DOE′pan-ax   LESS′own-eye, but more commonly, sue-doe-PAN′ax)
Common Name: False panax
Nativity: New Zealand

If you've had trouble with, or lost a few, *Scheffleras* (umbrella tree), try this beautiful and hardy substitute. Unlike the umbrella tree, which it resembles, it is pest-resistant and durable. Scales seem to be the only predator which presents a problem with this species but, because of the contrast of the foliage, they can be easily seen and dealt with. *P. lessonii's* foliage is somewhat blunt-tipped and partially serrated (see illustration), deep-green in color and leathery in texture, usually five leaves to a branch. You will see a hard, shiny residue covering the grow-

ing tips from time to time. This is a natural resin produced by the plant and not, as you might think, honeydew excretions from some parasite. This residue sometimes can deform new leaves and, if you can remove it without damaging the leaf, this should be done periodically. It grows fairly rapidly in an upright, tree-like (which it is) fashion to about twelve feet indoors and to twenty feet in its native habitat. I particularly favor this plant for two reasons: (1) It seems willing to thrive just about anywhere except dark corners, and (2) it responds to topping off by invariably branching two to five times, giving it a fuller, more attractive appearance. Suckers appear frequently at the base of the plant and compensate for the loss of lower foliage as the plant develops a trunk and matures into a tree. **Price:** At the nurseries in California, Florida and other temperate areas, you can

Pseudopanax lessonii (False panax)

find *P. lessonii* in cans. Prices range from $2.25 to $3 for a gallon can and $6.95 to $9.50 for a specimen in a five-gallon can. These are usually under lath and will adapt indoors virtually overnight. Potted specimens range anywhere from $6.50 for a plant two-feet tall up to $125 for a nine to ten foot specimen with several plants in the pot.

Basic care: A basic soil mix kept on the dry side is best. Let the soil dry out to a depth of two inches before irrigating again. Favors bright natural light—sun filtered through a thin curtain, for example—but adapts easily to lower light levels. Growth may slow in dim light. Temperature requirements are those in which you are comfortable. Needs good ventilation above 80° and doesn't like excessive chilling in winter. Mist daily to raise humidity spring to summer. Feed monthly April through August with a complete fertilizer at half strength.

Rhapsis excelsa

(RAP′sis ex-SELL′suh)
Common Name: Large lady palm
Nativity: China

This is another of the traditional outdoor tropicals still routinely used (often as a substitute for bamboo) in temperate areas as a landscaping plant. It has several features which make it an ideal houseplant. First of these is its attractive appearance. Its trunk has some of the characteristics of bamboo but is covered with brown, fibrous leaf sheaths. Its deep green, fanshaped foliage resembles, from a distance, the leaf pattern of the *Schefflera*. Closer examination reveals striations in the leaves. The leaf tiers are carried on slender, delicate-looking stems. Other desirable features are its affinity for shade, which makes it a logical choice for interior use; its tolerance of dust and drought; and the fact that it seldom achieves heights above five or six feet, which makes it easily manageable indoors. One other benefit is *R. excelsa's* slow-growing characteristic, which means

Rhapsis excelsa (Large Lady Palm)

repotting is seldom necessary more often than every third or fourth year. It is beneficial to replace the topsoil and some of the bottom soil every two years, since a plant that is not potted on with fresh soil soon depletes the nutrients in the original potting medium.
Price: Usually, a potted specimen is available in a four-to-six inch container for $4.95. Mature specimens which have achieved full height average $75. This figure varies and is higher or lower depending upon the type of container, number of plants in the pot, type of outlet, etc.

Basic care: A basic soil mix is suitable, but an extra couple of handfulls of leaf mold are beneficial. Likes continually moist (not wet!) soil, even damper than most other houseplants. This is especially true during the summer months, if kept in an unairconditioned environment. Frequent misting is also helpful. The normal interior temperature ranges are fine, but *R. excelsa* can take the higher ranges much better than the lower. By and large, a spot which receives bright, diffuse light is ideal, but this species is tolerant of much lower illumination levels. Direct sun (except in winter) has a tendency to yellow-off or bleach color from the foliage. Feed monthly from spring to fall with a complete fertilizer at half-strength.

Solanum pseudo-capsicum
(sol-AN'um SUE'doe CAP'sih-come)
Common Names: Jerusalem Cherry
Nativity: South America and Europe

Jerusalem Cherry, like poinsettia, usually makes its appearance in early December as a colorful plant to brighten holiday tables. The usual practice is to discard the plant after its fruiting season, since it is an annual, but it can be salvaged and carried on by hard pruning and repotting in early spring. It can also be pruned and planted outdoors in mild areas of the country. The plant produces long, glossy leaves to four inches and white, fragrant, star-shaped flowers half an inch wide. These give way to red or yellow fruits which resemble cherries or small tomatoes. Since these fruits are often poisonous, those with very small children (who are usually willing to try anything that even remotely looks edible) should pass on this one. With plants brought along from year to year, new growth should be pinched out periodically until summer to promote a fuller specimen. A height of four feet is tops with this species, and three feet is average. **Price:** Normally, only available in pots. Prices range from $4.95 to $15, depending upon the size of the plant being offered and the outlet.

Basic care: Thrives in a basic soil mix kept barely moist during its heavy growth period, then slightly dry. Allow the soil to dry out between irrigations. Can take 80°+ day temperatures, but requires a sharp drop at night. Prefers a night level around 50°-55°, although

you probably can get by with 60°. Maximum winter sun is called for and even likes some morning sun in summer. Bright natural light may suffice. Feed in spring and again in late summer with a complete fertilizer at full strength.

Spathiphyllum floribundum
(spath-ih-FY'lum flor-ih-BUN'dum)
Common Names: White flag; Peace lily; Spathe plant
Nativity: South America

Since the *S. floribundum* is a flowering plant, it really has no place in a book on foliage houseplants. but, because of its affection for water, high heat and its blooming quality in very low light, I've arbitrarily included it. It develops dark-green lance-

Solanum pseudo-capsicum
(Jerusalem Cherry)

shaped leaves that begin right at the soil line, which makes it difficult to prune out damaged or dead foliage neatly. But, its crowning glory is its delicate white long-lasting flowers (spathes) which unfurl suddenly from what appeared to be leaf stems. It can burst into bloom anytime of year, especially in winter when its flowers are most appreciated. Although the plant is easily divided to increase your stock, division often ruins the appearance of a showy specimen, reducing it to several mediocre plants. It requires two things to do well—"tight shoes," or a pot that seems too small in relation to the bulk of foliage, and fairly high humidity, which keeps the leaf tips from browning off. **Price:** Seldom available in cans. Most specimens are offered in six-inch pots at $6.95 to $8.50. Larger plants are priced accordingly. Select one that has set buds, if you can. One that is already a

Spathiphyllum floribundum (Spathe Plant)

riot of blooms has just gone through a flowering cycle.

Basic care: Use a basic soil mix laced with extra sand to promote fast drainage. In summer water daily; in winter, every two days. If ever there was a water-loving plant, this is it, but never let it sit in a bog. Light requirements vary from specimen to specimen. Although it abhors direct sun, it does well in or near a bright window. It frequently thrives and blooms in near total darkness. It prefers the upper ranges of the temperature scale: 85°+, but can survive in normal comfortable household temperature levels. Feed weekly during spring and summer with a complete fertilizer at half-strength. When blooms fade, cut them back as close to the soil line as possible. New ones will soon appear.

Stenocarpus sinuatus

(steno-CAR′pus   sin-you-AH′tus)
Common Name: Firewheel tree
Nativity: Australia and New Caledonia

This beautiful tree is still virtually unknown as a houseplant. You probably won't, for example, find it in your local plant boutique, but you may find it at your nursery. It adjusts indoors better than many conventional houseplants, provided you can give it a spot which gets bright natural illumination. In its native habitat, it grows to about 35 feet with a 20 foot spread. Obviously, it won't attain anywhere near this kind of height indoors, even if you wanted it to. It will reach the ceiling, though, in a few years, if you start with a plant in a five-gallon can. As a small juvenile, it produces large, deep-green, leathery leaves lobed like those of the oak tree, thickly set on its branches. Leaves are often a foot long, but seven inches is the average. Older, established trees bloom, producing striking red and yellow flowers which are structured like the spokes of a wheel, thus the common name, "firewheel tree." Begin pruning the tree the first year to achieve the structural shape you desire, or simply let the plant grow naturally. **Price:** If found in pots at plant shops, $10 would be a fair price. Nurseries offer specimens in cans for $2.50 to $3.95 for a gallon can and not much above $9 for a five-gallon can.

Basic care: S. sinuatus thrives in an acid soil to which you add an extra trowel of sand to promote good drainage. Keep the soil slightly dry—water when the soil is dry two inches down. Humidity isn't important, but a weekly misting or wiping down of the broad leaf surfaces improves their glossiness and removes dust from the stomata so the plant can "breathe." Temperature levels aren't crucial; a night range of 55°-60° and a day range of 70°-80° are suitable. Most do best in a partially-sunny window or nearby, but a bright natural light situation is acceptable. Eventually, the plant may be moved to dimmer light, but it's better to wait until the second year. Feed with a complete acid fertilizer diluted at half strength in April, June and early August.

Stenocarpus sinuatus (Firewheel Tree)

Tolmiea menziesii
(toll-ME'uh   MEN'zuh-see)
Common Names: Piggyback; Mother-of-Thousands; Youth-on-Age
Nativity: Alaska to Oregon

Currently a favorite hanging basket specimen, the piggyback is one of the few native American plants cultivated for indoor use. It is a hardy, creeping herb (of the Saxifrage family) which can reach two or three feet in height with an equal foliage spread of leaves five to six inches wide. It is the leaves which make the plant something of a novelty and give it its common names. New leaves grow mysteriously out of the old and send out roots which anchor in the soil. Once this is done, the mother leaf withers and dies. Leaves can be removed any time of year and rooted in moist sand or perlite, then potted up to increase your stock. Whether you propagate from the leaves or not, pinching out some of

them occasionally keeps the plant bushy and productive. If the plant is grown in good light it produces tiny green and brown flowers seasonally. **Price:** Hanging baskets range from $7 to $25, depending on size and outlet. Potted plants are generally priced from around 79¢ for a piggyback in a three inch pot all the way up to $30 for a large, well-grown specimen in a ten or twelve inch container. A medium-sized plant should be available for $3.95 to $6.

Basic care: A basic soil mix kept evenly moist is recommended. The plant deteriorates rapidly if the soil becomes too dry. Water should be kept off the hairy leaves. Moisture on the foliage may induce mildew or other fungi to develop. Depending upon the kind of light the plant was grown in prior to your acquiring it, T. menziesii thrives in partial sun, sun filtered through a thin curtain, or bright natural light. Most do well with bright light . . . south window, for example. Usually, piggybacks prefer the cool temperature range—50°-65°—but most adapt rapidly to average interior levels. In the higher ranges, the plant may flag and wilt, so cross ventilation helps. Feed in April, June and August with a complete fertilizer at full strength.

NOTES ON PRICE STRUCTURE: Most plants are priced on the basis of availability, size and the retailer's mark-up. The prices quoted are average, at the time of publication. Undoubtedly, one can find a particular specimen for less than the price listed and, conversely, for more, depending upon the source.

Tolmiea menziesii (Piggyback Plant)

Glossary of Horticultural Terms

Alga (AL'jeh) pl. **Algae** (AL'gee) Simple chlorophyll-containing aquatic plants that, with certain fungi, make up the Thallophyta, the first great group of plants. The fungi forms often grow on leeched-out salts on damp terra cotta pots.

Amendment (uh-MEND'ment) In soil, a conditioner which changes the character and texture of soil. Some common amendments are peat moss, manure, perlite, vermiculite, pumice, and sand.

Bromeliad (broh-MEE'lih-ade) Tropical American and South American genus of perennials which are members of the pineapple family.

Chelating agent (KEE'late-ing) Any chemical that makes nutrients, such as iron, immediately available to a plant.

Chlorophyll (KLOR'o-fill) Green coloring matter in plants.

Chlorosis (kluh-ROE'sus) A plant condition characterized by paling of normal green color to yellow, resulting from a loss of chlorophyll.

Complete fertilizer One which contains all three primary nutrients: nitrogen, phosphorous, and potassium.

Cuttings Sections or pieces of a plant severed from the mother plant and inserted in water, sand, peat moss, soil or other rooting media. When cuttings root, they are potted up and eventually become mature plants.

Cycad (SY'cad) Ancient palm-like plants, such as the so-called Sago palm.

Deciduous (dee-SID'you-us) Used to describe any tree or shrub which loses its foliage with the advent of fall.

Degradable (dee-GRADE'uh-bull) Capable of being reduced in amount or strength.

Dehydrated (dee-HY'dray-ted) Lacking in sufficient moisture. Characterized by wilting foliage and collapse in plants.

Dormancy (DOR'man-see) A usually brief but vital period of "rest" and inactivity for a plant which permits it to rejuvenate. Excessive cold may prolong dormancy, even though a plant may be ready to "break."

Dry well In pots without drainage holes, a layer of crocking, gravel, pebbles or other material in the bottom into which excess water may drain, thereby obviating soured soil and root rot. In saucers, a dry well of pebbles is often used to provide a beneficial microclimate and raise the humidity around a plant.

Evergreen Any plant which retains its foliage year-round is an evergreen.

Feeder roots The tiny thread-like roots which branch out from the main roots and collect nutrients to sustain a plant.

Foliar feeding, fertilizing A system for "quick-feeding" a plant in which nutrients are sprayed on the foliage where they are absorbed.

Friable (FRY'uh-bull) Descriptive of soil condition in which the soil, although moist, retains a loose crumbly character and resists packing.

Genus (GEE'nus) pl. **Genera** (JEN'er-uh) A plant group, consisting of a subdivision of plant family and groups of closely-related species having similar structural characteristics. The first word in a plant's botanical name is the *genus*, the second word indicates the kind or *species* name. For example, *Ficus* is the genus to which all figs belong and *benjamina* tells you what kind of *Ficus*.

Hardpan As the name implies, a sub-surface layer of soil whose particles are so packed together that it is virtually impenetrable. This condition is common when plants are potted-up in extremely fine soil devoid of fibrous material, such as peat moss or bark. Overhead watering over a period of months compacts the soil into the consistency of hardened cement.

Jumping Moving a plant up to a pot too large for its root structure.

Knocking out Removing a plant from its pot to check the condition of its soil or roots. (See Index for technique)

Larva (LAR'vuh) pl. **Larvae** (LAR'vee) The first stage of metamorphosis of an insect after leaving the egg, usually worm-like.

Leeching (or Leaching) In terra cotta pots, the action of moisture and minerals passing through the porous clay sides of the pot.

Leaf mold A high-nutrient-value mixture of decaying leaves, bark, soil, and other organic material which accumulates naturally over the years at the base of deciduous trees, or which can be made artificially by composting.

Loam (LOME') Soil that is a mixture of both clay and sand and contains some organic matter.

Microclimate (MIKE'roe-clie-mut) A climate within a climate. Specifically, a climate of a small area which is different from the surrounding climate because of certain conditions. For example, a plant whose pot is sitting on water-covered pebbles is existing in a microclimate created by the higher humidity level of evaporating moisture from the pebbles.

Mother plant The parent or donor plant from which propagations are taken.

Mulch (MULCH') Material, such as leaves, manure, leaf mold or straw, which is spread over the surface of the soil around a plant or tree to hold in moisture and prevent roots from drying out.

Offset An infant plant which grows from the base of the mother plant and can usually be separated for propagation.

Organic fertilizer Generally, all fertilizers whose sources are animals or plants. The sources include the various manures, blood and bones, fish and fish oils, tobacco, and peat, to name a few.

Osmosis (oss-MOE'sis) In biology, the absorption of one liquid into another through a thin membrane. Water collected by a plant's roots is passed through the semipermeable membranes of plant cells one by one. This process is called osmosis.

Palmate (POL'mate) Of plant foliage, divided like the fingers and palm of a hand.

Panicle (PAN'ih-cul) A loose diversely-branching cluster of flowers.

Peat moss Composed primarily of decayed sphagnum moss.

Photosynthesis (foto-SIN'theh-sus) The complex process by which a plant's foliage uses sunlight as energy (and chlorophyll as the catalyst) to manufacture sugars and starches from carbon dioxide absorbed from the air, water, and inorganic salts. The word "photosynthesis" is derived from two Greek words: *Photo*, meaning "light" and *Synthesis* meaning, "to put together."

Pinch back, out Removal of new shoots or buds, and sometimes entire branches, before they develop either to shape a plant or to encourage fullness and branching.

Pot-bound A condition in which the roots of a plant have developed to the point where they are crowded together, twisted and matted, and are unable to function normally. Plants should be checked periodically and potted on long before they become pot-bound, except in rare cases in which certain species thrive in a root-crowded condition.

Potting on Moving a plant up to a larger pot to provide adequate room for continuing root development.

Propagate To increase the number of plants by rootings or cuttings or several other methods, such as seed cultivation.

Respiration The process by which plants assimilate oxygen and expend carbon dioxide and water vapor.

Root-bound (See Pot-bound)

Root crowding A technique for encouraging greater foliage growth and faster maturation in plants in which the roots are confined for a time in containers too small for the root structure, thereby forcing a plant to transfer most of its energy to leaf development, rather than root expansion.

Root rot A condition, usually brought on by excessive water in the soil, but sometimes by certain fungi, in which the roots decay and die. This is always fatal to the plant.

Rosette A clustering of foliage growth similar to the petal structure of a rose in which the leaves seem to radiate out from a central point in overlapping fashion.

Salts Sodium nitrate which is used as a source of nitrogen in fertilizer production.

Sphagnum moss (SFAG′num) A moss-like plant that grows in bogs which is highly water-absorbent and is used as a mulch, propagating medium, and soil amendment.

Stoma (STOH′muh) pl. **Stomata** (STOH′muh-tuh) Minute orifices, or "pores," in the epidermis of leaves which enable a plant to carry on respiration and/or transpiration.

Succulent (SUC′you-lent) Any of the fleshy, water-storing plants of the desert and arid places of the world. The very name, *succulent*, means, "full of juice," which aptly describes this plant group.

Sucker A shoot that develops from the soil at the base of a plant, instead of from the stem.

Systemic (siss-TEM′ic) Affecting the entire system. For example, a systemic insecticide is taken up by the roots of a plant and carried throughout its system, from the feeder roots to the tips of the foliage.

Trace elements Chemical elements which are needed in small amounts by a plant for it to flourish. These are calcium, magnesium, sulphur, iron, manganese, boron, copper, and zinc.

Transpiration A naturally-regulated process by which excess water (in vaporized form) is expended by the leaves of a plant through the stomata.

Index

A

Acer palmatum, 77
Adiantum pedatum, 69
African milk tree (*E. hermentiana*), 101, 103
Agave, 11, 53
Allium schoenoprasum, 62
Aloe americana, 53
Aloe filifera, 53
Aloe stricta, 53
Aloe victoriae-reginae, 53
Anethum graveolens, 62
Angelica, 59, 63
Angelica archangelica, 63
Anise, 59, 60, 61
Anthriscus cerefolium, 62
Aralia elegantissima (*D elegantissima*), 99
Aralia sieboldii (*F. japonica*), 105
Araucaria excelsa, 11, (Description and cultivation requirements), 81
Artemisia dracunculus, 63
Asparagus ferns, 11, (Description and cultivation requirements), 81
Asparagus meyerii, 81
Asparagus plumosus, 81
Asparagus retrofractus, 81-83
Asparagus sprengerii, 81-83
Australian laurel (*Pittosporum tobira*), 11
Avocado, 78

B

Baby tears (*H. soleirolii*), 11
Bamboo, 77, 121
Bananas, 78
Basil, 61
Beaucarnea recurvata, 11, 83, (Description and cultivation requirements), 84
Begonia, 69, (Description and cultivation requirements), 84-85
Benjamin tree (*Ficus benjamina*), 105
Borago officinalis, 61
Boston fern (*Nephrolepsis exaltata*), 11, 12, 99, 114
Botanical gardens, 14
Bottle gardens, 65-71
Bottle palm (*Beaucarnea recurvata*), 11, 84
Bougainvillea, 77
Brassaia actinophylla, 12, (Description and cultivation requirements), 85-87

C

Cactus, cacti, 11, 27, 28, 30, 37, 44, 53-57
Cannabis, 99
Caraway, 60, 61, 62
Carum carvi, 61
Catnip, 63
Century plant (*A. americana*), 53

Chamaecereus silvestri, 66
Chamaedorea elegans, (Description and cultivation requirements), 87, 89
Chervil, 59, 60, 62
Chinese rubber plant (*Crassula argentea*), 96
Chives, 60, 62
Chlorophytum comosum, 88, (Description and cultivation requirements), 89-90
Cholla, 56
Christmas cactus (*S. bridgesii*), 57
Cissus antarctica, 11, (Description and cultivation requirements), 90-91
Cissus rhombifolia, 11, 73, 90, (Description and cultivation requirements), 91
Codiaeum, (Description and cultivation requirements), 91
Coffea arabica, 77
Coleus blumei, (Description and cultivation requirements), 92-95
Cordyline stricta, (Description and cultivation requirements), 95-96
Coriander, 60, 63
Coriandrum sativum, 63
Corn plant (*Dracaena massangeana*), 99, 101
Corypantha elephantidens, 55, 56
Corypantha vivipara, 55, 56

Crassula argentea, 54, (Description and cultivation requirements), 96
Croton (*Codiaeum*), 91-93
Crown of thorns (*Euphorbia milii*), 11, 103
Cycadaceae, 97
Cycas revoluta, 11, (Description and cultivation requirements), 96-97
Cyclamen, 11
Cygon (Dimenthoate), 48

D

Dehydration, 45, 46
Dieffenbachia, 7, 10, 11, 19, (Description and cultivation requirements), 97-99
Dieffenbachia amoena, 97
Dieffenbachia picta, 97
Dimenthoate (Cygon), 48
Dizygotheca elegantissima, (Description and cultivation requirements), 99
Dracaena, 11, 95
Dracaena marginata, 9, (Description and cultivation requirements), 100-102
Dracaena massangeana, (Description and cultivation requirements), 101-102
Dragon tree (*Dracaena marginata*), 9, 101-102
Dumb cane (*Dieffenbachia*), 11, 96, 97
Dwarf date palm (*Phoenix roebelenii*), 116
Dwarf mandarin orange, 77

E

Echeveria, 53, 55
Elephant-foot tree (*Beaucarnea recurvata*), 84
Elkhorn (*E. l. cristata*), 103
Enchinopsis, 56
Epiphyllum, 56
Epiphytic, 56
Etiolation, 46
Euphorbia, (Description and cultivation requirements), 103
Euphorbia biglandulosa, 103
Euphorbia caerulescens, 103
Euphorbia canariensis, 103
Euphorbia hermentiana, 101
Euphobia lactea, 103
Euphorbia lactea cristata, 103
Euphorbia milii, 11, 103
Euphorbia pulcherima, 103
Euphorbia splendens, 103
Euphorbia trigona, 103

F

False aralia (*Dizygotheca elegantissima*), 99
False panax (*Pseudopanax lessonii*), 119
False sea onion (*Ornithogalum caudatum*), 115
Fatsia japonica, (Description and cultivation requirements), 105
Fennel, 63
Ferocactus, 56
Ficus, 11
Ficus benjamina, 9, 44, 74, (Description and cultivation requirements), 105-107
Ficus carica, 77
Ficus elastica decora, 107
Ficus lyrata (*Ficus pandurata*), 9, 105, (Description and cultivation requirements), 108-109
Ficus retusa nitida, (Description and cultivation requirements), 109

Fiddleleaf fig (*Ficus lyrata*), 9, 105, 108, 109
Fig tree (*Ficus carica*), 77
Firewheel tree (*Stenocarpus sinuatus*), 123
Fittonia, 69
Foeniculum vulgare, 63
Frilled fan (*Euphorbia lactea cristata*), 103
Fuchsia, 11

G

Gardenia, 11
Genera, genus, (Definitions), 125
Geraniums, 77
Glochids, 56
Goldthread (*C. trifolia*), 69
Grape ivy (*Cissus rhombifolia*), 11, 91

H

Haworthia, 53
Healing onion (*Ornithogalum*), 115
Helxine soleirolii, 11
Hens and chickens (*S. tectorum*), 54
Herbs, 59-63
Honeydew, 50, 51, 119
Howea belmoreana, 11, (Description and cultivation requirements), 109-111

I

Indian fig (*O. ficusindica*), 56
Indian laurel (*Ficus retusa nitida*), 107, 109
Ixora, 11

J

Jade tree (*Crassula argentea*), 11, 96
Japanese aralia (*Fatsia japonica*), 102, 105
Japanese maple (*Acer palmatum*), 77
Japanese yew (*Podocarpus nagi*), 118
Jerusalem cherry (*Solanum pseudocapsicum*), 121
Jungle cacti, 56, 57
Jungle flame (*Ixora*), 11

K

Kalanchoe, 53
Kalanchoe pinnata, 53
Kangaroo vine (ivy, treebine; *Cissus antarctica*), 11, 89, 90
Kentia palm (*Howea belmoreana*), 11, 109, 116

L

Large lady palm (*Rhapsis excelsa*), 121
Lime tree, 77
Lobivia, 56

M

Madagascar dragon tree (*Dracaena marginata*), 101-102
Maidenhair fern (*A. pedatum*), 69
Mammillaria, 56
Mango, 78
"Marijuana plant" (*Dizygotheca elegantissima*), 99
Marjoram, 62
Marjorana hortensis, 62
Mealybugs, 12, 14, 48, 49, 50, 89, 95, 96, 102, 103, 114
Medinilla amabilis, 111
Medinilla curtisi, 111
Medinilla magnifica, (Description and cultivation requirements), 111-113
Medinilla teysmannii, 111
Melissa officinalis, 61
Mexican breadfruit (*Monstera deliciosa*), 113

Milk-striped Euphorbia (*Euphorbia lactea*), 103
Mock orange (*Pittosporum tobira*), 11
Monstera deliciosa, 10, 107, (description and cultivation requirements), 113-114, 116
Mother-in-law's tongue (*Dieffenbachia*), 97
Mother-of-thousands (*T. menziesii*), 124

N

Neanthe bella (*Chamaedorea elegans*), 87
Nepeta cataria, 63
Nephrolepsis exaltata, 11, (Description and cultivation requirements), 114-115
Norfolk Island pine (*Araucaria excelsa*), 11, 81
Notocactus, 56

O

Ocimum basilicum, 61
Olive, 78
Opuntia, 56
Opuntia ficusindica, 56
Opuntia microdasya, 56
Orchid, 11
Orchid cacti, 56
Oregano, 62
Origanum vulgare, 62
Ornithogalum, 115
Ornithogalum arabicum, 115
Ornithogalum caudautum, 115
Ornithogalum narbonense, 115
Ornithogalum saudersiae, 115

P

Painted-leaf plant (Coleus blumei), 93
Palm lily (*Cordyline stricta*), 94-95
Papaya, 78
Parlor palm (*Neanthe bella*), 69, 87
Parsley, 60
Partridge-berry (*Mitchella repens*), 69
Peace lily (*S. floribundum*), 122
Peanut cactus (*C. silvestri*), 55
Peperomia, 69
Philodendron pertusum (*Monstera deliciosa*), 113
Philodendron selloum, 12, 74, 115, (Description and cultivation requirements), 116
Phoenix roebelenii, 77, (Description and cultivation requirements), 116-117
Piggyback plant (*T. menziesii*), 123-124
Pigmy date palm (*Phoenix roebelenii*), 77, 116, 117
Pimpinella anisum, 61
Pincushion cactus (*Mammillaria*), 56
Pipsissewas (*Chimaphila*), 69
Pittosporum tobira, 11
Podocarpus, 117, 119
Podocarpus maki, 117, 119
Podocarpus nagi, (Description and cultivation requirements), 117, 119
Poinsettia, 103
Polypodium vulgare, 69
Pony tail (*Beaucarnea recurvata*), 11, 84
Prickly pear (*Opuntia*), 56
Pseudopanax lessonii, (Description and cultivation requirements), 119, 121
Pteris, 69
Pyrethrum, 50

R

Rattlesnake plantain (*Goodyera pubescens*), 69

Rhipsalidopsis, 57
Rhapsis excelsa, (Description and cultivation requirements), 120-121
Ribbon plant (*Chlorophytum comosum*), 89
Rose grape (*Medinilla magnifica*), 111
Rosemary, 60, 62
Rosmarinum officinalis, 62
Rubber tree (*Ficus elastica decora*), 10, 107
Rudolph Roehrs (*Dieffenbachia cultivar*), 97

S

Saddle-leaf philodendron (*Phiiodendron selloum*), 12, 116
Sage, 62
Sago palm (*Cycus revoluta*, 11, 96
Salvia, 62
Sanguisorba minor, 63
Sansevieria, 11
Schefflera (*B. actinophylla*), 9, 12, 85, 87, 105, 119, 121
Schlumbergera bridgesii, 57
Scleratium delphinii, 47
Sedum, 11, 53
Sedum morganianum, 53
"Self-heading" philodendron, 116
Sempervivum, 54, 55
Sempervivum tectorum, 54
Sentry palm (*Howea belmoreana*), 109, 111
Solanum pseudo-capsicum, (Description and cultivation requirements), 121
Spathiphyllum floribundum, 20, (Description and cultivation requirements), 121-122
Spider plant (*Chlorophyum comosum*), 88-89
Split-leaf philodendron (*Monstera deliciosa*), 10, 107, 116
Springtails, 47
Star pine (*Auracaria excelsa*), 81
Stenocarpus sinuatus, (Description and cultivation requirements), 122-123
Stripe-leaf dracaena (*Dracaena warneckii*), 101-102
Sword fern (*N. exaltata*), 114

T

Tangelo tree, 77
Taragon, 63
Terrarium(s), 19, 65-71
Thyme, 60, 63
Thymus vulgaris, 63
Tolmiea menziesii, (Description and cultivation requirements), 123-124
Trailing arbutus (*E. repens*), 69
Tree philodendron (*Philodendron selloum*), 116
Trichnocereus, 56

U

Umbrella tree (*B. actinophylla*), 10, 12, 85

V

Vermiculite, 35, 36, 37
Vitus anarctica (*Cissus antarctica*), 90

W

Water (requirements of for plants), 27-33
Weeping Chinese banyan (*Ficus benjamina*), 105
Weeping fig (*Ficus benjamina*), 9, 105
White flag (*S. floribundum*), 121-122
Wintergreen (*P. elliptica*), 69

Y

Youth-on-age (*T. menziesii*), 123-124